PORTRAITS & REPETITION

Library of Congress Cataloging-in-Publication Data

Ratcliffe, Stephen.
    Portraits & repetition / Stephen Ratcliffe.
        p. cm.
    ISBN 0-942996-46-1
    I. Title: Portraits and repetition. II. Title.

    PS3568.A717 P6 2002
    811'.54--dc21   2002042549

Cover drawing by Etel Adnan

Book design by Simone Fattal

The Post-Apollo Press
35 Marie Street, Sausalito, California 94965

Printed on acid-free paper in the United States

PORTRAITS & REPETITION

Stephen Ratcliffe

THE POST-APOLLO PRESS

PORTRAITS & REPETITION

ACKNOWLEDGMENTS

Some of these poems have appeared in the following:
American Letters & Commentary, Aufgabe, Combustible Void, Conjunctions, Conundrum, Duration, EMPTY SET, Facture, First Intensity, Flux, LIT, local howler, Lungfull!, Melodeon, non, New American Writing, Pavement Saw, Phoebe, Pink Squid, Poetry and Plural Identifications, Skanky Possum, Shiny, Syllogism, VeRT, Walrus, Windhover, and *26.*

Thanks to the editors for their support.

I began to wonder at at about this time just what one saw when

one looked at anything really looked at anything. Did one see

sound, and what was the relation between color and sound, did

it make itself by description by a word that meant it or did

it make itself by a word in itself.

— Gertrude Stein, "Portraits and Repetition"

2.9

green plane of the ridge more bright than before, (<u>position</u>)

of sunlight in following line being what actually happens

how the mind turns back on itself, first person on the bench

(elsewhere) far away remembered in relation to two others

reflections of landscape below sky in water (psychological),

shape of the person in blue smiling on the opposite shore

picture where the sound of driving begins, (order) on a road

between fields of thought and the inside edge of the page

one is writing for years a letter, or listening to the sound

(passing) of white birds landing in the field on the left

2.10

blue towel in the window where light (otherwise) would come,

foundation upon which one feels the other's common ground

what became of the telephone view, opposite rooftops (field)

including the position of water and/or islands and bridge

how little there is now between them, the bridge washed away

(observation) and the phone lines down where a tree falls

man having approached the woman at the airport for instance,

planting a kiss like her father's (memory) on right cheek

whether it's possible to walk outside in the dark, otherwise

to be still in a chair (calculus) or stretch on the floor

2.11

legs pulled back in bed waking (paradigm), in which the body

thinks the other person won't be present in that position

clouds stationary above the horizontal line (process), whose

shapes in that case will be understood as a form of music

(example) scrawl on the envelope addressed to second person,

the hand itself as different as its mark in that position

accident when the car pulls away (calculation) into traffic,

the appearance of men believed at first to be threatening

vowels clipped at the end of his name in Denmark (magnitude)

for instance, the window next to the door bathed in light

2.12

waking to moonlight through the upstairs window, the picture

(proof) someone is missed as the absence of legs entwined

wallet (<u>exact</u>) also missing, when the person who picks it up

disappears toward an adjacent room in the following frame

letter not wanting to be sent at a given time (<u>attitude</u>) not

because an action isn't happening but to whom, about what

sound of water (picture) becoming another music on the roof,

before which the body rolls over into its now empty space

envelope propped against window glass as before, the address

scratched in pencil (reversal) instead of the actual face

4

2.13

notation in the classic introvert's hand mistaken (<u>movement</u>)

at face value, as sun climbs through haze of next morning

(<u>technique</u>) of placing one sound after the other, or hearing

when the words in uncertain weather move in from the west

sequence of notes instead of numbers descending on the page,

(position) whose record of that event continues to repeat

hole in the clouds moves the whole sky, which itself appears

to be the case (empirical) depending on whether one looks

doing what angels are said to do on the page, the man writes

to the sounds of invisible birds out the window (<u>without</u>)

2.14

starting up on the left in grey and white (sound), the green

perception of tobacco plant leaves from which water drips

woman at the table in a sequence of tones, who isn't reading

a book in which action is about to take place (procedure)

sunlight as clouds open on the white of a page whose subject

moves to his left, (condition) then farther away from him

marriage in the sense of not being (<u>this</u>), relation to woman

walking toward the door somewhere to the right of the man

sound instead of its absence in the field, view of car (<u>not</u>)

visible in southwest corner of the park walking around it

2.15

sound in the woodstove now that it's morning (logic) sparks,

the stray cat walking toward a place in the sun next door

shadow of a leaf cast on the white wall adjacent to this one

which doesn't change because there isn't wind, (sentence)

(thinking) notes in music Bach transcribed, the second after

the first lifting like a feeling toward a different pitch

two bare feet placed on the green cover of a book, intensity

(surface) of green in relation to green of actual leaves

where the cat sits against the neighbor's wall, pile of wood

in the foreground (picture) beyond which water then drips

7

2.16

lavender in the window in a tall cylindrical vase (contrast)

left of the bird on the page, upon which water is falling

action of moving the rock (sequence) to man's left, position

of the seated bronze figure now prominent because of that

other person calling back from beyond the edge of the ridge,

having left the room in the present (<u>defined</u>) like memory

two-dimensional surface of the second picture (<u>that</u>) texture

of green, how certain plants can be pulled up by the root

piano (here) instead of strings on guitar, when sound itself

arriving from the next room can be heard in terms of that

2.17

water moving underground, light becoming the subject (logic)

at the conclusion of the next sentence following this one

above the ridge beyond which window (visual) it can be seen,

repetition of a sound analogous to the sense of its place

silhouette of a plant slanted against it, which isn't to say

another action doesn't happen in the next frame (meaning)

(example) girl being disturbed when she phones in the night,

having missed seeing or possibly speaking to him about it

motion going faster as the notes ascend, or so it might seem

to the listener approaching from adjacent room (position)

9

2.18

stone (index) on the window sill, woman arrived from another

country in terms of which a given picture has been framed

not looking out across buildings, roofs extending (gestures)

horizontally into the almost palpable Mediterranean light

same woman at a table on the beach facing forward, the ocean

at her back (figure) flat blue and suddenly very far away

whose face isn't seen (pattern) though not turning away, who

won't thus be recognized for the actions she doesn't take

landscape observed from a plane in the distance, after which

she declines to say what's happened (possible) or is felt

2.19

calling back or writing instead of it (<u>proof</u>), letter itself

not the same as something she is feeling driving in a car

curled edges of the white flower against glass, beyond which

leaves of tobacco plants (number) as green motion in wind

voice interrupted by static on the wet street, what it means

to have met the second person for instance (<u>fact</u>) for tea

cut of grass viewed from above, whose lighter color of lines

is registered as the texture inside its surface (pattern)

staying in another city with other men, which isn't the same

(<u>shape</u>) as calling to say what has and/or hasn't happened

2.20

raindrops on the roof (physical) now that a tree has fallen,

which lies out in the dark potential of its sound's shape

car then stopped in a ditch, not going further down the hill

(possible) or forward in some opposite sense of direction

condensation on the window through which sun's light (image)

has arrived, how such a person is thinking to start again

sound of frogs when it gets dark, this diagram of horizontal

black bars on a white ground after echo of which (figure)

(one) water in the large curve of the bay this next morning,

where another distant sound recedes as if without a trace

12

2.21

three enormous flowers opening against the window, where red

(shape) of the unfolding petals is analogous to genitalia

how many pins the woman thinks to stab into the man's (<u>five</u>)

picture, after how many times then ripping it into pieces

narrative continued in telephone space, which isn't actually

the subject of anger but hearing about it (demonstration)

(frame) not to have experienced it before like that, so also

man not knowing whether to place it in the picture or not

edge of cloud moving up from the south, the person meanwhile

(<u>situation</u>) who calls back from the other end of the line

2.22

shape of a blue flower in the window (<u>same</u>) which was placed

there by a second person, coming back from somewhere else

small white spider who tries to hide, right (angle) of stalk

below which drops of water are passing from unconcealment

outline of two rocks adjacent to one another before (figure)

this view, where sunlight makes up for the missing person

whether to be alone in such a room or drive toward the sense

that someone is willing to be spoken to, place (<u>imagined</u>)

(note) curled edges turning brown, where the weather changes

the presence of a smell and sound descending will be felt

2.23

analysis of the relation between horizontal lines (division)

illustrated in figure 3, rain pouring from edge of a roof

how the woman on a walk to the park (<u>chain</u>) falls to pieces,

which isn't what the man was feeling in a different place

texture of water before the wind comes up from the southwest

quadrant, position (<u>point</u>) of view when driving toward it

body visible below the surface, not as notes or the silences

between them but as a form articulates (<u>internal</u>) meaning

meanwhile (unfolds) the same red flower, as a random pattern

in black and white on granite rock in the middle distance

2.24

lattice of suddenly bright adjacent to shadow (relationship)

on a table, glass through which motion of leaves casts it

woman in bed waking up (physical) for example, sexual action

in the dream repeated as actual situation instead of that

bend of a road between two planes, curve of body in position

before the second person falls back to sleep (penetrated)

(apparent) white of a cloud's shape moving in from the north

above which field of blue, as weather changes its meaning

grid of lines extending beyond a picture's rectangular space

(define) for instance, which Mondrian intended to suggest

2.25

half (counting) white plane of sky, in which nothing matters

speaking about where she will put the children and things

narrative of broad green leaves in motion, (<u>think</u>) of deer's

footprints in the just-turned soil not being there before

second person calling back at seven (<u>ambiguous</u>) as expected,

as if a conversation could replace what actually happened

overlapping surfaces of a color receding into the background

which isn't separate, subject walking toward it (perhaps)

not motion but absence of it, what she thinks left of center

(structure) after the picture plane is turned on its side

2.26

angle of sun directly at eye level, how it appears (<u>present</u>)

the moment the person looks out from the upstairs window

who isn't moving toward the house, prospect of car returning

on a road the driver has chosen instinctively (<u>empirical</u>)

glimpse walking past it of the pink rose in the cypress tree

it climbs, the angle at which (sense) the tree might fall

voice in the reading (picture) an assumed voice, this person

choosing to be heard or not depending on who is listening

sound of birds overhead on a wire, below which water (think)

pours from a pipe's mouth somewhere to the right of music

2.27

gap between the physical word and the object in relat

to the person who doesn't call, named elsewhere (though\

(number) letters in series scrawled on the page, as if shape

of the actual body of water could be made present in pond

landscape in two dimensions spelled from left to right, body

moving above or through it (figure) a material phenomenon

telephone calls in the night (position), first person silent

in response to what the second says being lost in thought

four lines with four words of four letters in four different

colors (act), interrupted by the present call of the crow

2.28

. . . what are poets for in a destitute time, Heidegger asks

moving from across the page toward unconcealment (action)

(<u>margin</u>) phenomenon of sun rising through a screen of leaves

prior to acoustic shape of birds in field, sound of notes

spelling phonetically, how does she know if the person's dog

(experiment) is asleep in the picture whose space is real

iris still the color of the painting in the vase (physical),

the difference between the shape of weather and its sound

suddenly a new space, next image of the reader's head moving

in shadow (<u>arbitrarily</u>) across warmer colors in the floor

3.1

(knowledge) as oblique angle of vision on the object itself,

how the painting frames the world in which she moves away

hand in motion hanging up the phone (gesture), not perceived

but in letters approximate elsewhere to what has happened

not wanting to experience (negation) the sound of his voice,

earlier frame assuming a presence of gaps between silence

what she says having answered the phone, grammar of a letter

something like the feeling color also suggests it (means)

(impression) six or seven different sounds of birds outside,

surface of glass below which lavender seeds lie scattered

21

3.2

shapes of the 'm' and 'n' in 'moonlight' being and not being

equal, which is like moonlight the viewer thinks (itself)

(one) waking to sound repeated of a crow in the cypress, not

a fact of attention as much as the thing itself suspended

figure in room who sits as the mind clears itself of thought

(function), ideas of mimesis in which other action occurs

landscape extended in whatever direction one looks (single),

metamorphosis of the 'd' into 'p' also therefore possible

understanding, her feeling in hearing the sound of his voice

that something inside the brain (object) had been touched

3.3

heads dropped, the palest of pink-white flowers (transition)

beside a postcard depicting his attempt to locate himself

man facing the figure on a couch (known), how she is dressed

in black and white with pearls to punctuate the intensity

behind words the grammar of thought, her desire to interpret

failure of action in what doesn't take place (phenomenon)

(difference) between one person and another, 'you' and 'she'

because of which the woman imagines something is possible

condensation the moment he looks up, green beyond the window

(impression) after which the child waking with his mother

3.4

reflection of trees in water (surfaces) symmetrical to trees

beyond it, appearance of leaves beginning at first breath

solitary, person thinking about the woman reading the letter

(position) driving home after hours of not falling asleep

hearing and seeing at the same time words like (<u>proposition</u>)

'things,' objects lined on the opposite edge of the table

subject missing, (<u>other</u>) person in that case wanting someone

to witness what she intends to say concerning his absence

purple of iris adjacent to rose pink, inner speech continued

as sunlight climbs above the horizon (<u>single</u>) one is told

3.5

light grey rather than bluer light, the way a letter printed

(angle) is said to create sound as much as be its product

order in music the same as order which controls the feathers

in a bird's wing, the person on the phone saying it (<u>ear</u>)

(contradiction) of the woman wanting things returned, figure

at table opposite an arrangement of black and white notes

same person almost driving off the road in that light, shape

transformed (<u>sentence</u>) into act of attention to the world

each letter an action in the landscape whose third dimension

is sound, the absence of color in the first place (blank)

3.6

vertical lines of water as temperature outside a glass warms

(angle), small dark birds flitting back to cypress branch

such difference between silence and empty space, perceptions

of moments in patterns the eye sees (series) as ear waits

arrangement of colors in grid, red-white of an enormous bulb

beyond which the green-blue plane of the ridge (diagonal)

(therefore) gap between lines like silence, a sense of words

written down vs. escaping and/or somehow being taken away

assumption that certain things have been returned (picture),

ascending order of notes concomitant with thinking itself

3.7

duration of the white space between words (<u>abstract</u>) silence

or empty sound, the bird startling up from clump of grass

rose fading in foreground (imagine), wall extended into near

distance against whose glass surface grey of sky reflects

(<u>opposite</u>) a figure of informed passion the notebook itself,

notes for instance played in the order of the composition

statuette of a Buddha whose arms stretch overhead (<u>entirely</u>)

possible in one sense, the bronze collected in meditation

sound in a line a memory of its physical shape, shape itself

also a memory of sound (<u>system</u>) spoken or otherwise heard

3.8

figure walking away through glass (<u>difference</u>), the way wind

appears in its absence to be moved from elsewhere into it

pillow of fog on bed of ridge above which composition's grey

white, where form is the point of what's seen (<u>predicate</u>)

(<u>this</u>) going back to events as if memory of writing anything

on paper makes it happen, the person returning her things

which doesn't mean there isn't a feeling, actions at the end

(<u>expression</u>) of a series of mistakes determined before it

resonance of cello solo, purples of new wild iris positioned

in front of a robin (<u>concept</u>) who continues to look right

3.9

piano (method) instead of a silence in the room, hand moving

diagonally away from a body she has also decided to leave

positioned between lines of dried black and white fish, face

(direction) behind which a list of words beginning with d̲

density of greens through which sun rises, where the soprano

imitates the person whose husband isn't there (confusion)

(structure) followed by wind, red quarter-moon in blue field

pulled from upper left to lower right corner of a picture

spacess between letters moving physically from this position

(etc.) to that, motion of leaves the echo of wind passing

3.10

pattern in water of the wave whose green-blue surface breaks

in fact, actual figure (impression) climbing down a cliff

evidence in words of actions taken, what she means or thinks

she means saying she also wants a witness (x) for closure

list of titles including NW winds variable to 15 knots, lows

in the mid teens and twenties in the mountains (question)

(count) sense walking back from water that birds echo shape,

figure still crouching under the pitching lip of the wave

Belle of Portugal climbing up the tree, dried petals (1 + 1)

fallen from place above a glass at the edge of the table

3.11

(suppose) now light of sun behind a pine bough, line between

being inside experience and its memory as echo of a sound

subject waking in the middle of the night (after) wind waves

to 2 feet, swell west 5 feet instead of actual perception

number the other half of a double image interrupted by phone

(1 . . . 9) call, low tone of his voice speaking of which

form of person's head moving as shadows over color of floor,

where that person stands for the woman missing (variable)

(example) text of quotations, sense of numerous unseen birds

in the picture to the left of more distant ambient sounds

3.12

road in dark minus traffic (logic) empty, placement of table

as car swerves remembered as letters arranged to enact it

woman not in bed, not walking out the door with her suitcase

(<u>example</u>) starting then to walk across the just-cut grass

girl in the preceding scene actually half-dressed, afternoon

sunlight at windows of room whose feeling reflects (<u>that</u>)

(measure) feeling back, muscle pulled in water as it pitches

over the man viewed from down the line inside to the left

nothing said as to what or why what happened happened, woman

disappearing into right margin (<u>this</u>) which doesn't speak

3.13

conscious in another room of traffic (addition) then another

voice through the wall, figure arrived in different place

body (comparison) whose head tilts back, appearance of smoke

in upper left hand corner meaning she has breathed it out

perspective below window of abstract landscape whose primary

feature is water, therefore pattern of wave (grammatical)

(knowledge) of three lines translated into two, what happens

after the man starts to walk toward her in memory of that

sound as echo or memory of physical shape repeated, not that

(expression) of object in the sentence can't be obsessive

3.14

first in this order ('language') punctuation of bird sounds,

vertical columns of sun cast through blinds onto far wall

lighter color green of different water facing west (picture)

as consequence of this, driving in taxi meaning to see it

flesh after twenty-three years in the ground which no longer

covers Yorick's skull, play's penultimate scene (example)

(empirical) contrast Tarzan swimming in the jungle pool, how

soon he will save Jane from certain black and white death

instead of the clinical name for a genital organ, the father

(transition) who doesn't seem to appear except as a ghost

3.15

memory of air on body (position) different from its feeling,

as sound prior to writing what doesn't happen takes place

arrangement of figures at the table read like word on a page

rather than object, lily closest to the viewer (physical)

($\underline{x}$) still life of flowers in the lower left foreground, view

parallel to the picture's plane being part of the subject

glass flask on the shelf within which clear liquid (example)

of the woman's condition, man in room that starts to spin

place of body (logic), division of painting into seven parts

based on division of the flower that is again its subject

3.16

violins (abbreviation) at sunrise 6:18, which doesn't happen

given the texture of a low cloud banked against far ridge

how when the man enters his sense of direction (co-ordinate)

changes, orange globe on the table where nothing had been

triangles of neighbor's roof bisected by vertical red stripe

of chimney, front door key lost in moonlit grass (aspect)

(series) patches of light blue sky overhead, color of actual

red and white lilies at a window standing only for itself

another possible frame, rose-pink petal of just-picked Belle

adjacent to an earlier form of low tide (calculation) 1.6

3.17

memory of woman turning toward the second person (<u>different</u>)

in back of her, standing beside man in white on the right

wind in bamboo moving outside glass (transition), horizontal

surface of water building to ten feet at fourteen seconds

body no longer in the same room, person who watches the rose

(<u>method</u>) fade between the sound of one note and following

emotional contiguity of a bird landing on left branch, music

analogous to feeling of the subject in the door (measure)

(<u>system</u>) of sound, events like action listed in random order

concluding with figure whose back turns toward the window

3.18

man walking on bricks around a corner of the house (forward)

as sun lights ridge, which order of action doesn't matter

cello in third movement more impossibly beautiful, the curve

of the first calla reaching opposite right (construction)

(result) previous event, sun disappearing into cloud horizon

accompanied by equally slow motion sound of winds off sea

utter simplicity of its connection (system) to it, a subject

whose shadow pedals at the same speed some distance ahead

red moon in a blue field on the table adjacent to (calculus)

Cranach the Elder, a bird in foreground standing for what

3.19

antler beside the oranges and the book, (<u>that</u>) space between

objects similar to the one between one letter and another

alternations of notes in descending order syncopated (<u>there</u>)

against feelings, which thus may be heard by the listener

oranges spilling from bag imagined in place of actual fruit,

whose position on the right (<u>exact</u>) nonetheless continues

woman waking up not knowing it (<u>possible</u>), the second person

wanting to be the masculine subject in a following clause

actions taken louder than language itself, plane of one body

(<u>condition</u>) moving opposite to the direction of the other

3.20

color in front of color in painting of enormous (<u>experience</u>)

flowers, man driving closer to a condition of seeing that

former views of buildings in grid, grey sky below which wind

(<u>language</u>) begins to change what occurs in the foreground

woman in front seat facing forward as durations of syllables

heard, conversation defined in terms of that (<u>empiricism</u>)

(<u>step</u>) green flecks of cut grass scattered on brick, feeling

her head then moving close enough to be in a word touched

shoulder exposed in place of empty bed, the way sound opened

a picture of two people in darkness (<u>how</u>) conscious of it

3.21

first day of spring (<u>fusion</u>) grey morning, increasing clouds

the chance of rain more abstract than sound of it falling

two adjacent rocks on top of the third flat one (<u>realistic</u>),

curve of the smooth body form of description in name only

upstairs now in bed, how the second person becomes an object

(psychological) calla lilies turn their necks to look for

notes in Bach's Sarabande Four numbered in sequence 1-5, his

pupils reflecting how the woman gazes at them (<u>attention</u>)

(<u>a</u>) abandon all hope you transcribed, which appears possible

in light of the woman who is beginning to wake beside him

3.22

radio sounds to the left of which (<u>describe</u>) a pair of white

callas entwined, iris in window faded from green to brown

color of shirts in closet, scene closes with view (opposite)

of ridge in the overcast light of wind from the southwest

birds' wall of sound also perception, first shoulder covered

in a pale word whose feeling is of being present ("blue")

(<u>effect</u>) parenthesis also moving from line to line, a memory

of reader at window reclining on pillows the color of sky

presence of a second body felt by the other, which is subtle

as much as a physical act (symptom) or the sound it makes

3.23

coincidence of word and feeling it echoes (mental), how that

person leans back to answer the girl who asks her to stay

lute transcribed for the piano as background to this, (<u>this</u>)

scene on the ridge in which the man gets lost in the dark

subject moving toward a conscious decision in (<u>order</u>) to see

which is possible, wind sound in highest cypress branches

how it might not be so, another's response as measure of her

own perception of a landscape prior to green (<u>experience</u>)

(theory) word's sound a memory of its physical shape, itself

echoes the sound of a bird behind the roaratorio of ocean

3.24

wind from southwest (<u>without</u>) being felt, proximity of Venus

to waning eighth-moon whose curve as the sky lights fades

(describe) landscape of buildings, the first person thinking

of moving present situation to the next or following line

round table in window inevitably followed by second thoughts

(<u>essential</u>), idea taking place after the color of morning

seeing the angle of light above a cloud (<u>more</u>) now, in front

of which motion of plum branch whose leaves have come out

person walking up the path toward pink-white camellia (<u>this</u>)

after which she becomes 'you,' sun now emerged from cloud

3.25

film of a window through which the man sees shapes (someone)

not moving, the subject opposite not yet driving in a car

clouds (<u>none</u>), space under a house made larger than previous

picture suggests descending through the hole in the floor

overlapping of multiple voices ascending on a scale of notes

remembered, as if color could itself be heard (<u>immediate</u>)

(<u>before</u>) sudden intensity of sunlight above the pine branch,

after which the random arrangement of petals on the floor

birds whose enthusiasm isn't seen, rock leaning against wall

between panes of glass whose role (<u>function</u>) is to answer

3.26

horizontal lines on a far hill above which curves (possible)

of ridge, person across metal table facing somewhere else

sounds of water falling in the night (<u>indirect</u>), paler color

of buildings muted by where a particular green absorbs it

who sits in front of the man being washed, angle of shoulder

(number) decreased by pressure of hand placed on the left

birds landing on a branch of another tree behind which white

clouds passing in blue sky, a person (<u>who</u>) is also moving

closeup in previous scene (<u>what</u>) of how green buds come out,

how such a view will arrange the space of sound it echoes

3.27

time of day (<u>content</u>) attended by curve of a particular leaf

through glass, bird's pattern of flight landing in a bush

nothing else in mind until the next word approaches (<u>actual</u>)

position of clouds in sky moving from northwest, abstract

first scene again (<u>only</u>), four rows of five circles opposite

pictures of what happens when the woman gets into the car

how when she listens more closely a pressure in the left ear

in second picture, sunlight through pine branch (another)

(series) pictures in sequence, not just the notes themselves

but objects moving in the foreground when a breeze begins

3.28

shadows through window of new leaves on branch (<u>spontaneous</u>)

the top of which extend beyond the picture, which matters

where buildings stand, (<u>what</u>) person upstairs aslant the bed

remembered as the sound of letters made to look like that

cat paused on the counter that doesn't sound, object between

source of light and its appearance (form) on a white wall

bird anchored on a tip of right branch (<u>counting</u>) now three,

one possibility being to hear the sounds of present space

(<u>concept</u>), green of calla lily stalks through water in glass

made to look larger than where they cross in air above it

3.29

five green stalks instead of two in a glass, water's surface

below which the subject's feeling can't be seen (optical)

(that) evidence the highest part wants a firmer touch, hands

on piano meaning to double the melody in the lower octave

rain falling as a cloud moves from northwest (this) position

above water, figure inside crouched under lip of the wave

which is (seeing) memory, shadow of the man's head reflected

in window as profile on the wall behind him being present

blue heron stalking towards nearly visible waterline (theme)

also past, letters side by side suggesting something else

3.30

another weather system, receding views of porch seen through

bamboo grid of vertical lines (example) before light hits

subject's arms (<u>empirical</u>) marked red, where the rose's form

pruned branch by branch becomes a shape in the background

clouds not moving otherwise above pattern (memorize) of sky,

whose blue at that instant is made more emotional as such

(<u>picture</u>) bodies asleep next to one another followed in next

frame by grey light before sun rises, no birds then sound

perspective looking out above woman's position in landscape,

horizontal areas of blue-green (<u>forms</u>) representing ocean

3.31

buildings in middle distance beyond (<u>reversed</u>) condensation,

sequence of four figures in foreground about to disappear

letters ('constructed'), hole in floor through which the man

descends spelled like this fact of events in actual house

clouds in previous scene (<u>not</u>) present, a syncopated pattern

of apparently random drops spilling from grey-white field

new leaves on a branch from which the bird taking off curves

away, (<u>this</u>) sound a physical sensation of water in pipes

now two returned (<u>assertion</u>) where nothing or one was, space

between viewer and rectangle of building on opposite hill

4.1

voice on stairs behind (head) of boy, whose presence doesn't

mean the subject isn't visible if the man is looking back

(another) after a second glass watching the man on a pillow,

conversation about which anything more or less isn't said

new mass of branches moving from the other direction (<u>over</u>)

the sound it makes, horizontal shape of bridge beyond it

missing floor amplified by absence of wall in adjacent room,

the woman's figure composed of cylinder and cone (<u>sphere</u>)

asleep in the bed (<u>less</u>), now thinks back to crowd of people

two of whom explain how long their marriage hasn't lasted

4.2

rose-pink glow in sky above irregular line of trees on ridge

changing, (<u>one</u>) after which the sun rises at 5:54 exactly

two rocks adjacent on top of third (<u>objects</u>) also as before,

bodies coming into the presence first of one then another

edges of clouds below which a bird flies west suddenly light

(again), wind from northwest not yet moving green of leaf

seeing inside the dark seeing itself, the woman as she turns

toward the person beside her (one) who is himself present

concept (<u>applied</u>), how the sun may be said to light the edge

of ridge beyond where branches in foreground intersect it

4.3

how upstairs the person is (particular), listens to the bird

elsewhere the instant its sound ascends to bedroom window

rain coming to consciousness first as notes on roof (<u>there</u>),

three-note call of the song sparrow after which its trill

blue glass on sill then blank of grey-white field beyond it,

green plane of ridge below sky becoming horizon (picture)

(<u>picture</u>) shallow wave gauge three feet, the occasional gust

more than enough to rattle the window in an adjacent room

source of light behind weight of cloud cover, how it happens

(<u>what</u>) which places the music as an echo in such an event

4.4

reflection of man's head in glass (<u>here</u>) outside looking in,

shapes of the buildings in the darkness beyond it all lit

reading (means) the text of the world, words like the sounds

it makes echoed when the person sees it crossing the page

glimpse of three red buds about to come out (note), observer

walking along the path below them on his way back to work

tongue in lover's ear, after which first one person (object)

then the second falls into a suddenly dream-induced sleep

saturated yellow of wall in smallest room, grey light beyond

plum trees outside (<u>this</u>) series of rectangular buildings

4.5

cloud (proposition) below plane, white shape of the mountain

between a point of departure and word whose music follows

sparrows in a green book diving (<u>inside</u>) circle, man sitting

in relation to jasmine in the window and branch beyond it

simultaneously waking, mouths in the night turned toward one

another's direction (opposite) without beginning to think

notes overwhelming the meanings of words in that sense, what

happens when one voice rises above another (mathematical)

(perspective) which isn't sound of a bird in the foreground,

as if she were the echo of someone who is herself thought

4.6

pairs of wings rising out of what appears to be (<u>mean</u>) blank

landscape, piano on the radio persistent as recorded past

wherein person gets up, room darker than previously imagined

and clock (<u>there</u>) which doesn't advance beyond ten-thirty

watercolor clouds against which three birds (proof) continue

curving away, what the reader of the words alone can hear

feeling behind lines (example) the eye sees moving from left

foreground, drops of water falling from the tip of a leaf

shovel stepping into earth itself, woman on the right moving

in slow motion through outside gate (<u>analysis</u>) toward him

4.7

15 feet 17 seconds, (<u>not</u>) shape of ridge beyond condensation

on windows through which nothing significant will be seen

(<u>after</u>) missing floor taken up again, man in blue crawl suit

disappearing under the southeast corner of the foreground

woman now hearing a series of reasons <u>not</u> to move, listening

to reading (<u>image</u>) of words that spell sound of the world

coincidence of sunlight below pine branch (<u>original</u>) motions

of leaf, the person opening the door the better to see it

separation of strands of sounds which include birds, weather

in no particular order following (<u>construction</u>) its music

4.8

flash of light on a stair wall, man walking down in the dark

(between) concept of a line and hearing something outside

highest point of building (intension) above which the planet

swims, which is itself framed in picture of opposite roof

parallel lines of sky as if cut between clouds before light,

being visible as it climbs after the sun rises (equation)

(part) two figures in a crowd, one leaning back as the white

of the subject moves above green plane of middle distance

series of receding vertical planes outside (form) of a hill,

previously included in the feeling of looking in a mirror

4.9

acoustic drone of weather (equation) radio in the background

analogous to shape of letters, jasmine on the window sill

bed where the shovel cuts through grass, path between bricks

(movement) series of rectangular planes in relation to it

violins descending into a sequence of horizontal forms (it),

irregular curve of low clouds on ridge above which a bird

frogs outside in the night, condition of bodies (understand)

which rise to the surface of a pond whose water is opaque

(all) still, hole in the floor in front of the door opposite

arrangement of matches whose presence the picture records

4.10

two descriptions (<u>that</u>) white flower in a blue glass at left

edge of window, contours of buildings in shadow on a hill

bird which lights on a single plum branch then leaves (<u>now</u>),

the meaning of the frame contained inside imaginary ridge

syntax of clouds moving across page of the sky, illustration

of such weather a possible subject (<u>only</u>) when read aloud

(<u>what</u>) image followed by what is seen, man behind the camera

to the left of the woman who doesn't see him turn to look

cloud behind which sun lights still moving from south, (<u>how</u>)

an arrangement of points below blue field also isn't seen

4.11

flat grey light (a) sky in which nothing can be seen, memory

of the sound the person inside listening to reading makes

(this) green in contrast to how it climbs ridge beyond whole

field of others, another seen as if seeing it in the dark

woman in aubergine not equal to someone standing in doorway,

panorama (p) of shadows in the second half of description

moving back and forth between parents (must), vertical right

margin parallel to green and blue bars on front room wall

meanwhile the sound of birds around a corner in cypress tree

for instance, repetition of notes (this) page on a screen

4.12

planet before the appearance of light nearly vertical (<u>such</u>)

above point of building, clouds not above band on horizon

shape of painting not described in telephone call by the man

whose mother is dying, weather in the second line (<u>clear</u>)

(example) distance between diagonal lights on opposite hill,

traces of the pen visible from the other side of the page

color in the room a warmer shade of white, faint as the star

after light increases (<u>calculate</u>) being less than visible

birds on a plum branch (<u>p</u>) beyond which the horizontal line,

sun approaching a verbal event in relation to what we see

4.13

turning back across the room (A) to where the figure gets up

in the dark, paper wedged at side of door where it closes

(<u>following</u>) surfaces, contour of leaf in the middle distance

between figure in window and shapes of clouds breaking up

how as the sky turns light a point of light (<u>defined</u>) fades,

moving southwest as it climbs above rectangular buildings

bird departing from vertical branch of the plum which itself

(<u>determined</u>) thus moves, second person entering the third

sound the echo of thought (<u>form</u>) or feelings, the upper edge

of a cloud near the horizon suddenly starting to light up

4.14

twenty degrees below normal (example) snows above 3000 feet,

grey-black shape of clouds to southeast just below planet

pink-white head of rose bending from glass in window (form),

whether its color is the same or if not fades toward what

sounds of birds in cypress tree (description), whose silence

continues as the physical texture of feeling behind words

suggestion of ridges through film of moisture in the window,

above which sky has cleared as it grows light (empirical)

(one) clock beside a piece of granite on top of which pieces

of fossils, wind in the motion of the branch out the door

4.15

bird landing in the field to the left of the viewer, another

(number) somewhere above the window in the previous scene

gradual warming trend, silence interrupted when a car passes

in the street followed by a constant (<u>this</u>) song of birds

which (<u>isn't</u>) in the same key, the size of letters on a page

changed in the sense that a reader isn't likely to notice

place where the door isn't yet imagined, feeling on the back

of a picture (here) whose words have gradually faded away

missing a point of light (<u>that</u>) isn't the planet, increasing

as sun appears between a pair of invisible trees on ridge

4.16

left knee and/or right shoulder feeling motion (<u>that</u>) moment

exactly, light between the man and wall of adjacent house

present action on stage including these words, whose meaning

will be (<u>this</u>) sound the acoustic shape of letters spoken

map of nails on a white wall showing where each picture was,

water in the east next to (<u>these</u>) additional images of it

speaker asking "Who's there?" (<u>played</u>) in the dark, to which

the other person replies "Stand" instead of answering him

(<u>other</u>) events also off stage, the woman pulled down singing

under water preceded by the older man asleep under a tree

4.17

planet left of where the building (<u>is</u>) a point of perception

itself, the man waking from dream wanting not to remember

climbs higher, theory of weather which assumes that the wind

(<u>a</u>) starts the moment the sun rises proven not to be true

man standing formally to right of material plane (<u>a priori</u>),

called by someone else for instance the collector of cats

(<u>counting</u>) inches in the ceiling, perspective how one thinks

what happened elsewhere seen in words used to describe it

whether the wall is filled with pictures (<u>identity</u>) question

of place, faint now as horizon turns the lightest of hues

4.18

source of light behind a pine branch (<u>knowledge</u>), silhouette

of a bird landing between the viewer and right foreground

cat (<u>interpret</u>) stopped in a patch of sun on the blue floor,

another whose head casts a small shadow from doorway left

(<u>also</u>) memory, the man upstairs fixing the crack in the wall

when the woman walks in wanting to be noticed and touched

winds from the northwest gusting to 19, (<u>related</u>) phenomenon

of a rose-pink bud unfolding halfway up the cypress trunk

image of man's head (example) reflected on leaves in window,

the piano an acoustic analogue to the shapes of its notes

4.19

swell period 15 to 17 seconds (calculation), particular view

of the Belle's pink-white head drooping over edge of vase

planet (something) faint as a star when only one is shining,

specific length of finger above the pine's clipped branch

body moving beneath the man's which is itself moving, (form)

including possibility of children asleep in the same room

wind bending the tops of scotch broom in field whose yellows

are also therefore moving, ridge beyond that (understood)

woman whose body has wasted away (not) then breathing, child

arriving in the following scene to find himself an orphan

4.20

color of wall (phenomenon) changed in different light, thing

seen different from something said by characters on stage

film of clouds drifting down the stream of the sky, (action)

including sun rising at 6:28 with seas 13 feet 14 seconds

man taking off left of the person paddling up face of a wave

(position) exactly, which is then played in reverse order

(possible) picture, man walking into the room with shirt out

and tie on backward claiming he has come to take her body

which itself doesn't exist except as a memory, hollow of eye

and the skin pulling across absence of breasts (anything)

4.21

sound of how many birds (<u>qua</u>) bird outside, man opening eyes

in a particular light to make sense of what it is he sees

(<u>one</u>) instant the sun behind line of ridge followed by flood

of light on wall the next, shadow of a cup where none was

ceiling below which color of upper walls is a given (number)

something softer than white, which warms as light hits it

quarter waning moon moving to the right corner of the house,

its relation to line of clouds not present (<u>circumstance</u>)

(<u>this</u>) action taking place now, how smaller of two rose buds

on branch in a glass on window sill appears to be opening

4.22

grey wisps above horizon (<u>position</u>) above which second faint

planet approximate to first, moon's bright curve to right

point of building between reflected light, relation of color

(<u>that</u>) on the cover of the book framing the interior view

person whose things on back of car across the street include

pieces of watercolor paper glued in a grid, ('intuition')

(<u>what</u>) then becomes pink edge of grey, below which different

planes of rectangular white buildings begin to take shape

memory as the pale blue cast of thought of 'things' not seen

(<u>grammar</u>), how sentences serve to describe how things are

4.23

clouds driven north (n) above ridge, sound of window closing

upstairs a mixture of two white colors in the first place

not how the woman raises her legs in the dark but why (not),

gap between word and feeling of thing happening off stage

roar of ocean outside (first) followed by six drops of water

on the window, red between green of rose split apart more

two forms on orange blanket before the fire itself goes out,

position of head somewhere below the other's (mechanical)

(how) block of building against black of sky painting looks,

which is a difference between thinking and sound of pitch

4.24

eleven windows in an upstairs view (<u>one</u>), hills of buildings

between which flat grey plane of water seems to be moving

wind from south, ship traffic disappearing behind the corner

house in back of which rectangular edge (<u>this</u>) isn't seen

whether a certain white mixed with hint of oranges (<u>a</u>) looks

like that, planet still climbing above upper line of roof

(<u>new</u>) green leaves not present, a branch where rose was tied

higher up the cypress become the shape of words on a page

memory of sound (<u>consistent</u>) glass on the window sill, woman

on top of man who wakes to see lights before light breaks

4.25

how many pink-white globes opening against trunk (<u>analysis</u>),

how much color on the room's walls looks like sun's light

sound of birds again in front of the weather, "Who's there?"

in response to the play's seen but unspoken action (<u>here</u>)

(<u>not</u>) present, the woman's back below motion of other person

included in early view from beyond the sliding glass door

action said to be 'missing' except in sound of words, echoes

what first one then the other (<u>character</u>) will talk about

plane of ridge (<u>there</u>) not moving, flock of birds in whitish

sky above it not the color of the window's frame upstairs

4.26

no moon meaning most dark (fact) crossing rocks where bricks

will be, after which the man in the picture crawls on top

(this) the example of action performed, man who says "answer

me" already standing with back turned at Bernardo's words

gesture seen as body's pronouncement in terms of which sound

now heard, (how) blank space of sky into which sun climbs

elsewhere in black ink on its side opposite "Nay, answer me"

which doesn't (mention) the name of the man who says that

bird (means) its own sound, either shape of physical 'thing'

or the picture in words that takes its place for instance

4.27

woman walking up hill in first picture (assumption) breaking

into tears, which isn't part of the feeling of Rondo in A

two rose buds still (this) way, second leaf from left beyond

which leaves outside continue in random pattern of motion

(mathematical) pattern of bird sounds through closed window,

person waking up alone in the middle of a fog-bound world

color of frame around the door warmer than walls (appearing)

themselves, the word in its role in the text of all words

yellow for instance moved from left of front door to a table

in front of the window, west wing at viewer's back (more)

4.28

tadpoles at the opaque green surface of water in glass (and)

greens of the field beyond, to which they too will return

(so) soon, subject moving in another place away from the man

who continues to sit by window at table on the blue floor

grey-white film of air between the plane and ridge, is (not)

therefore visible except to the extent that one 'sees' it

source of light also missing, off stage to the right perhaps

as a series of actions which happens in words only (said)

(act) itself spoken and heard but not seen, bird for example

landing in cypress as a horizontal motion in blank of sky

4.29

blank where a building continues (<u>philosophical</u>) as absence,

angle thought to be part of what's missing in the picture

air that also isn't seen made visible in the motion dark red

adjacent to green of leaves, drift of weather (<u>essential</u>)

(<u>not</u>) sleeping, the person upstairs on her stomach who wants

second person not to get up or otherwise climb toward her

pale pink camellia next to another brighter one, (<u>different</u>)

intensities of warmth in patches of light orange on walls

word's sound (<u>logic</u>) an acoustic shape, relation of its echo

in the air to order of objects or feathers in bird's wing

4.30

triangle of reflected light in the window (<u>one</u>) an open book

on table, thinner vertical shape of corresponding feeling

(<u>two</u>) figures approximately next to one another in the dark,

first of whom starts from somewhere else suddenly present

continuous views of water below plane of cliff in flat, grey

light (point) in the distance where the first wave breaks

on stage, what 'happens' imagined as the sound of the person

to whom one is listening to reading in that case (<u>effect</u>)

table (<u>where</u>) white rose is, branches in the middle distance

bending whereas the flag on the hill drifts the other way

5.1

size of leaves (<u>calculation</u>) beside others in a green field,

words spoken by actors who move on stage as well as speak

what 'happens' elsewhere the following thing (<u>same</u>) as cloud

hanging down in front of ridge, which isn't itself moving

yellow in motion on left, a sound of water beyond stationary

shape of trees coincident with its visual presence (<u>this</u>)

(<u>this</u>) action described in words stripped of physical action

someone might take, the man's head turning toward the sky

confusion of certain feelings (<u>also</u>) next to hers, as moving

from one place after the change of direction a bird makes

5.2

grey-white embankment of a cloud above the ridge (<u>physical</u>),

busy old fool sun rising into wide open blue sky above it

(<u>interpreted</u>) in the line following that, person interrupted

in the perception of things a sentence serves to describe

who or what enters from off-stage left asking "Who's there?"

for instance, (<u>it</u>) before anything can be said or noticed

(<u>different</u>) setting, thirty windows in the room facing south

wall of building on the peak of whose roof a bird perches

arrangement of photographs on the sill of an adjacent window

each of which is 'elsewhere,' small girl in (<u>this</u>) garden

5.3

white in the first place (<u>possibility</u>) behind and/or against

grey in field of light blue, which isn't to say something

(<u>one</u>) perception, the pink of the climbing rose not the same

as the flowers themselves in the window beginning to open

memory a wedge of opaque green plane between brighter hills,

the position of squares of colored paper in a grid (<u>that</u>)

rhythm the acoustic 'shape' of words in air, whose (<u>nothing</u>)

physical itself continues as the echo of its visual sound

light (<u>reflecting</u>) through back of clouds, the person in bed

who turns without being moved by any related verbal event

5.4

mist between window and ridge which isn't seen, (<u>not</u>) itself

'difficult' but writing that is also listening to reading

object placed on the left wall against whose blank something

'happens,' woman who (<u>must</u>) continue walking out the door

instead of the landscape à Genève (<u>normative</u>) a pile of wood

in the middle distance, in which form itself is perceived

(<u>white</u>) wall behind which frame, horizontal color in the one

above the other one something like the feeling outside it

cloud in opposite direction lifting, where sky breaking open

lets light move at that point against its sound (<u>observe</u>)

5.5

band of bright yellow horizon (<u>conjunction</u>) just below upper

edge, whole painting itself approximate to somewhere else

thinking behind the words being music, imperceptibly turning

from the south as a cloud before weather changes (<u>choose</u>)

(<u>nothing</u>) according to plan, her passing him without looking

exactly toward what did or didn't happen the night before

which takes place as landscape, dark shapes of trees at edge

of field beyond which more distant ("A") shadows on ridge

simultaneity of sounds (surface) bird inside scale of notes,

person in the green car driving away without looking back

5.6

cloudy with a chance of light showers, light itself diffused

as it passes through the absence of color (<u>philosophical</u>)

(<u>proof</u>) that space in which sound is, variation of ascending

notes in the left hand continued in the following example

large blue field in lower right quadrant beside (transition)

a series of vertical blue and green columns, whose shadow

person looking (<u>this</u>) direction, the words in the foreground

when the telephone rings and/or cat skids around a corner

events prior to the present action being performed on stage,

(<u>something</u>) about the curve of grass stalks in glass vase

5.7

wedge of lighter cloud above clouds an illusion of ridge ($\underline{x}$)

itself, woman in man's shirt above nothing passing behind

what happens next (example), which isn't the sound of colors

where the rose echoes how it looks in a glass on the sill

("here") person who enters the first to speak, "Who's there"

both the place one stands and an imagined space elsewhere

grey-green surface of water on a table toward which tadpoles

rise, bird landing on bare stalk against (<u>wider</u>) panorama

followed by events in a system whose words lift into the air

(<u>interest</u>), person in a distant city picking up the phone

5.8

sense of the person suddenly absent (proof), who goes to bed

well before dark and/or wakes up hours before first light

blanket pulled to the position where the body slept (<u>exact</u>),

fabric of grey sky hanging in a fold of still green ridge

(<u>attitude</u>) deep red, a single flower in the middle of orange

poppies whose own color it stands out against in contrast

words performed in visible space, elsewhere which isn't seen

becoming itself an object in that acoustic event (action)

sentence as (<u>picture</u>) 'how things are,' image facing the man

who sees in it an arrangement of muted rectangular shapes

5.9

nine times nine (<u>movement</u>) the day after noon arrives, trees

beyond the body of water in whose surfaces shapes reflect

seas from the southwest 2 feet 17 seconds (<u>technique</u>), first

breath of air in motion of leaves from opposite direction

(<u>how</u>) blue looks next to blue itself, in which feeling isn't

so much of sky but the sound it makes elsewhere in a grid

nail in wall between rooms where pictures were (proposition)

moved, which is why the person chooses not to appear here

five pink roses in window, reflection in glass as light hits

fold of small petal (<u>without</u>) calling attention to itself

5.10

light before (sound) of unseen birds, pair of planets moving

above silhouette of pine branch opposite almost full moon

'things' apparent in the feeling of water in picture (<u>form</u>),

performance of missing action heard but not seen on stage

second or next perception not (equivalent) to the same note,

horizontal plane of ridge defined by line of fainter blue

white on page after which sign of repetition between thought

and the sound it makes, following object not noticed (<u>is</u>)

(<u>not</u>) person seen, areas of color on the left echoed by pair

of grey-green shapes whose feeling repeats a verbal event

5.11

wind waves to 3 feet, swell northwest to 7 feet (<u>thus</u>) woman

getting up after hours of not sleeping before first light

ridge framed by pair of adjacent white windows through which

it floats, (<u>same</u>) concept reflected in the following line

which is a perception of mental space (<u>thinking</u>), pond water

upon whose surface a piece of wood becoming a frog floats

(surface) fish lifted to the dock having swallowed the hook,

from which a smaller image of itself is beginning to come

rectangular shapes of indecipherable color below and/or left

of letters in column, this development of other (<u>picture</u>)

5.12

grey-white film of a cloud positioned below top of ridge (x)

from this perspective, y who wakes up having such feeling

(same) sequence of events taking place off stage before play

itself begins, man for instance turning over in his sleep

rain on roof an acoustic (series), shape of five small roses

in glass perceived in the time it takes to move from left

beside the granite rock in the window a picture of the lake,

trees in right middle distance casting shadow toward (it)

'therefore' (can) occur, rhythm of notes played on the table

accompanied by a random pattern of sudden showers outside

93

5.13

plane of rectangular building facing another opposite (<u>such</u>)

hill, irregular red mass of foliage moving in front of it

(<u>meaning</u>) this other view of ridge not there, whose position

out the window is accompanied by sound of birds and a car

glare on page of book reflecting what takes place previously

for example, now the woman hanging up the phone (<u>perform</u>)

table outside covered in plastic (<u>point</u>) of space, emptiness

of feeling in the room made more apparent by such absence

horizon changed, emotion of man who sees bird on bare branch

(<u>passage</u>) not moving until it flits off over his shoulder

5.14

slant of moon's light (<u>sequence</u>) falling on wall beside bed,

after which light fills a space already filled with sound

clouds moving from the northwest before dawn, (<u>this</u>) gesture

in place of things moved from house to back seat of a car

detail of woman in front of a mirror wearing only her shoes,

saturated yellow of wall and floor and the body (<u>picture</u>)

(pattern) of actions repeated, man who calls back apparently

not wanting to stop what happens when the car drives away

smaller of two birds circling crow by the cypress (<u>possible</u>)

outside left window, whose sound is an echo of that event

5.15

reference to the color of the sky assumed, grey-white planes

of buildings whose perpendicular faces it defines (<u>proof</u>)

(number) of steps up which the man returns certain 'things,'

the shadow of the woman walking in the opposite direction

branch in the foreground behind which the same dark red plum

breaks into motion, (figure) elsewhere turns into herself

pictures of children on the white floor (<u>possible</u>) now gone,

porcelain of wall framed by shade of trim around a window

light on opposite hill imagined as a series of relationships

(<u>shapes</u>), hue and value depending on position of observer

5.16

shape seen through through panes of glass outside (physical)

neighbor's house, who without looking back will disappear

(<u>possible</u>) arrangement of instruments on paper in the window

behind which image of a hill, music made by such 'things'

where she sits registered by what she (<u>thinks</u>), brushstrokes

of white cloud against pale blue edged with tinge of grey

hummingbird that lights on a wire fence adjacent for example

to water (<u>picture</u>), blue jay lifting from trunk of an oak

sun poking through grey-white clouds, another in slow motion

moving between areas of green in opposite direction (one)

5.17

alternation of lighter green branches in the middle distance

(shape), sound an echo of the song bird's visual presence

faint motion of wind stirring an edge of tobacco plant leaf,

window through which the man isn't seen looking at (<u>this</u>)

grid of buildings on hill opposite sketch in black and white

(<u>certain</u>), the other person not present in that situation

purple of bearded irises in front of blue rectangular fields

in which the painter sees the sound of the world, (<u>frame</u>)

(<u>situation</u>) following the reappearance of the younger woman,

yellow tint of glasses pulled back into black of her hair

5.18

(<u>what</u>) 'whoo' sound of owl among events first noted, the man

coming to consciousness next to presence of light in room

dip between silhouette of trees on ridge when the sun comes,

(<u>this</u>) simultaneous to perception of first wind in leaves

smaller of two shapes in cypress calling sharply (<u>see</u>) here,

which the crow takes as a sign to fly away casually there

location (<u>imagined</u>) where the rose in the window was, darker

pink of bud on left next to about-to-fall petals of other

man forgetting to look for trace of two lights in sky before

sun floods it, the woman elsewhere (<u>not</u>) thinking of this

5.19

legs on a tadpole at the surface of the glassed pond (<u>same</u>),

shape of tail disappearing into greenish opacity of water

(<u>chain</u>) of notes including the rising one, whose alternation

echoes the motion of scotch broom's yellow waving in wind

lines in white field standing for street or building or tree

(<u>fact</u>), which isn't the view at this point in the picture

direction of bird's landing on bare stalk in middle distance

now, small craft advisory therefore in effect (<u>calculate</u>)

(<u>now</u>) leaves, green ones of pink rose in contrast to a grass

at bending tip of whose stalk hangs the heart-shaped seed

5.20

note in the shape opposite its sound (<u>object</u>), which the man

reads before not falling asleep in middle of starry night

three yellow roses (physical) on kitchen table, before which

sun itself rises through film of clouds on crest of ridge

(<u>line</u>) between what happens and the letters used to describe

it, appearance of the foreground including a bird's sound

distance of feeling translated into feeling of hollow chest,

hieroglyphics on a screen (apparent) in light of the room

where clouds moving away from the north leave hardly a trace

of blue and yellow to the right of the roses, (<u>this</u>) grid

5.21

(<u>that</u>) position relative to person from which certain events

will not be heard, cloud in shape of dog running now gone

direction of bricks from (<u>one</u>) structure to the other, field

of related color on a flat plane called a simple solution

sun soon, distances between the subject and viewer (<u>measure</u>)

seen in terms of field across which eye travels to get it

woman in a series of letters asking the man not to come back

(perhaps), actions off stage therefore not seen by anyone

persistence of the bird's invisible note at random intervals

not caused by another event also not seen, (<u>call</u>) it this

5.22

grid in black and white the approximation of color (<u>present</u>)

in the first place, person on the bed flinging herself up

(<u>possibility</u>) of rose on tree beside blue field for example,

appearance of the object subject to place from which seen

girl on man's lap (<u>casualy</u>), man standing at the microphone

shifting the focus of attention to mouth sounding the air

blue feeling of the sky through which the wind passing bends

the tallest of grass stalks, into which light (<u>sun</u>) rises

(<u>thinking</u>) relation of birds to the sound they make at first

light, woman on plane between landscape and picture of it

5.23

feeling ('thought') before eyes open, sound of water outside

imagined in shapes of letters analogous to the fact of it

diagonal slant of cloud light (<u>one</u>) above line of the ridge,

in front of which a pair of birds seem to be disappearing

figure walking around corner of neighbor's house (<u>congruent</u>)

who isn't here, her place in the picture having no climax

(<u>position</u>) on top, feeling of legs wrapped around other body

parts which haven't themselves materialized at this point

series of green and blue and reddish shapes placed in a grid

below an apparent horizon of hills and painted sky, (act)

5.24

imbrication of bricks between whose gaps sand and mortar mix

(<u>language</u>), man on the ground not asking her not to leave

(<u>note</u>) departure, where warmth of porcelain-white wall isn't

interrupted by a collection of objects adjacent to window

phenomenon inside the frame of painting limited (experiment)

to geometric shape, head of girl turned over her shoulder

rose climbing the cypress against whose trunk pinkish globes

punctuate a series of photographs, which isn't (physical)

(<u>arbitrarily</u>) made sound of bird remembered after waking up,

flute and harpsichord following each other's parts around

5.25

sunrise 5:53, after which effect of light through grey-white

column of cloud whose action happens on stage (knowledge)

yellow of rectangular building (gesture) below white of line

between it and bright orange, petals falling on the table

bird in air, where the sound the crow makes moves through it

(how) without reference to an observer who doesn't follow

multiple images of the same tree placed at a different angle

which translates something of the tangible world, (means)

(somewhat) pink-white, the rose bending under its own weight

above color of sky against which other shapes can be felt

5.26

color of cloud above crest of ridge (<u>movement</u>) turning grey-

pink at this point, whose landscape thought itself begins

empty space where white slants between two patches of green,

three-sided wedge on top of (<u>one</u>) above which yellow sits

(<u>function</u>) color in such condition, water in black and white

falling on roof before blue or green comes into the world

actual moment a petal (<u>single</u>) falls followed by bird waking

next door, shoes on copper table opposite bricks on floor

random pattern of song sparrow's flight from corner to green

field to branch it stops on, materiality of word (object)

5.27

(here) notes on sound, how the piano moving in the next room

approximates the slow rhythmic motion of cloud from south

man carrying her 'things' up a series of stairs again, first

rain then the sky lifting above buildings on hill (there)

animal in black and white, pillow propped against brick wall

(sense) which corresponds to pattern the man walks across

patches of nasturtium orange (under) green of leaves on pale

green wall of neighbor's house, thus the texture of music

color of picture not known, name of birds also missing (one)

a moment in air above passion flower red on a green fence

5.28

upper left corner of table (surface) slanted below the sill,

composition of yellow and pink in various stages of decay

man walking around the corner of the house adjacent to color

above which cloud brushes against the ridge, (assumption)

(part) missing, curve of landscape in the painting analogous

to presence of the person who witnessed it but isn't here

edge of tobacco plant leaf after which (another) drop falls,

all but illegible 'scrawl' that can in fact be deciphered

unidentifiable trills of notes from somewhere beyond cypress

(single) instead of traffic, image of grey sky above city

5.29

shape behind the shapes of perceptible sound (<u>itself</u>), water

in the distance like wind in tree out the sleeping window

(<u>what</u>) happened elsewhere in words only, acoustic phenomenon

visualized as action of letters in relation to each other

weight of grey-white cloud hanging in which triangular plane

against background of darker trees on ridge, (<u>this</u>) place

(<u>positions</u>) taken, the man moving to the left when the woman

leaves the room without thinking she will never come back

sound of petal as it falls to the table (<u>blank</u>) heard before

seen, after which silence in contrast to occasional birds

5.30

blue plane of water in motion below line of horizon, (angle)

at which the fainter planet moves directly into the light

relationship between the visible shape of swells approaching

from the southwest corner of the window, two clouds (one)

(calculation) of fact, meaning of the first person's gesture

toward color of the body coiled in the middle of the road

piano adjacent to the opposite window not played (therefore)

silence, punctuated at regular intervals by clock in hall

actual dog in the next room imagined in terms of one driving

(another) in car, grasses bending against same blue plane

5.31

profile of cypress branch (<u>abstracted</u>) extended horizontally

into left window, frame within which grey water meets sky

which doesn't (<u>merely</u>) describe it, place where white breaks

above rocks connected to the acoustic image which follows

altitude of certain flowers whose intensity of color changes

in relation to the man who walks into it, hill (<u>opposite</u>)

(dimension) of spelled view, curve of grass against blue sky

through which the clouds continue moving in from the west

lavender behind and adjacent to the viewer whose perspective

is also therefore changed, line (<u>system</u>) clear to horizon

112

6.1

flatness of light in relation to line between opaque (<u>order</u>)

surface of water and the grey of sky it reflects, objects

(<u>here</u>) subject moving through a field of blue flowers, angle

at which the eye perceives it measured in number of steps

dark red poppy on bend of path between orange gate and door,

(<u>technique</u>) by which white milky fluid might be collected

yellow on upper surface of wingspan of the two birds gliding

from behind edge of ridge below this, (<u>not</u>) without sound

echo of shape, white of half moon imagined against the black

of background through which faint light appears (<u>concept</u>)

6.2

hummingbird stopping a moment at top edge of middle vertical

window before moving forward, (<u>this</u>) unknown bird's trill

arrangement of yellow petals on the left corner of the table

(<u>title</u>), which is perceived in relation to color on paper

sound, shape and meaning of words in performance for example

action in terms of what happens somewhere else (<u>calculus</u>)

(<u>picture</u>) of cloud body above line of ridge, position itself

being an event on a surface which can't otherwise be seen

wind not moving green leaves in the middle distance, sparrow

(<u>a</u>) the difference between thought and the sound it makes

114

6.3

hollow in clouds where the light appears to be moving, (one)

whose presence becomes the inverse between grey and white

place above shoulder ('x') which could be what the man feels

scraping against it, sanding the window adjacent to glass

(question) following, how before light the body turning over

becomes conscious of the first invisible bird in the dark

faint breeze in leaves looking up from image of pastel house

above driveway, water color ascending toward blue (count)

(1 + 1) two ducks flapping east toward the line of the ridge

below grey sky, action elsewhere understood as that sound

6.4

irregular edge of the cloud above the top of the ridge light

below which sun climbs (glance) higher, suddenly blinding

weather report, body of the brown bird bending (after) which

green outside the window in relation to foliage around it

rectangular shape of pale yellow building moving to the left

adjacent to sphere of tree, as if paint itself (is) thing

(variable) swainson's thrush calling from trees below space,

half moon waxing in what remains of still bluest distance

writing not mirage but detail of seeing, (a) curves of grass

stalks below the end of which wedge of triangular granite

6.5

rose-pink sounding between the dark of clouds parting, whole

range of other notes rising in the field somewhere (<u>else</u>)

(<u>example</u>) bird next door, lights in window viewed from above

meaning the person who wasn't present previously is awake

painting around the frame instead of looking outside (<u>that</u>),

apparently random motion of black and white across bricks

shapes of letters in the first place followed by (<u>this</u>) echo

of thinking that gives them shape, not any colors but one

quail body at the side of the road juxtaposed to the feeling

green leaves, (<u>how</u>) motion of crow calling back and forth

6.6

sound in the first place outside room, space defined (<u>model</u>)

by an absence of two or three birds up before first light

yellow of horizon across the top of a rectangular blue field

the dimension of which cannot be determined, (comparison)

wall (<u>sense</u>) empty of the image which describes the person's

interior world, notes on strings as bow pulls across them

faded where petals fell, first of three magnified stems bent

toward the viewer whose perspective is changed (<u>decision</u>)

(<u>number</u>) of days, weather present in relation to the painted

surface of building whose rhythm moves from left to right

6.7

man in a play called landscape followed by wall, (<u>this</u>) idea
continuous with weather through tomorrow above the passes

picture (<u>p</u>) in black and white, reading adjacent to circular
repetition of another voice elsewhere not taking a breath

carved box in the woman's hand after she gives it to the man
who still doesn't recall, familiar curve of writing (<u>not</u>)

(empirical), sounds of blue borage around which bees humming
in the line previous to lavender in the neighbor's garden

red-winged blackbird landing on a wire, (<u>sense</u>) of its color
in relation to shape as the body glides off into the grey

6.8

clouds pouring down the crest of the grey-white ridge (<u>what</u>)

visible, above which palimpsest of blue moving through it

(<u>first</u>) person on his knees on the floor, who has previously

descended an irregular line into canopy of dripping trees

view from above of distant landscape below water toward edge

which frames it, (<u>this</u>) syllable's weight pressing itself

pair of birds (<u>imaginable</u>), yellows of scotch broom in plane

above whose green wings suddenly curving around the house

pastel shape to the left of an apparently random arrangement

(<u>logic</u>) of buildings on hill, flowers of friendship faded

6.9

sound of missing woman's voice left as the subject (<u>defined</u>)

picks up the phone, thinks she's driven two days in a car

granite rocks toppled on square of bricks, surrounding grass

grown wild (<u>long</u>) before the mower moves against the lawn

feeling echoed as cello continues, clouds whose impenetrable

blanket covers the bed of the field facing observer (<u>one</u>)

(<u>series</u>) of events, second person not appearing in the dream

suggesting she has receded into the walls of a white room

blue in lower quadrant extending more than half the distance

(<u>calculus</u>) to yellow, a family of skunks below the window

6.10

black surface of second table in front of window (<u>different</u>)

facing the opposite house, man on the red bed not reading

adjacent vertical view to the right (<u>one</u>) toward green lawn,

feeling of margin determined by an absence of looking out

woman not in the room when the man arrives, emotion measured

as the distance he drives from blue of car (<u>number</u>) there

(<u>are</u>) birds outside window, perspective beyond left shoulder

toward the texture of cloud blanket above flat blue floor

color of woman's voice on pale blue phone behind the viewer,

sound (<u>system</u>) of white cloud above visible line of ridge

6.11

blank wall to the left of a field whose place in the picture

(somehow) changes it, small black birds on walk to closed

gate beyond which thinking at the center of a large concrete

square, (_imagine_) that place not touching the woman's arm

narrative of letters in woman's hand not sent from the city,

perch giving birth to live babies on the dock (_condition_)

('corresponds') to missing person, view of building from car

in which the man's gestures of moving aren't acknowledged

series of events repeated therefore (_exist_), the blond child

not the woman in a film but girl asleep beside her mother

6.12

crow on bare branch scolding its mate, red of tallest (<u>that</u>)

first poppy lifting its head through the waist-high grass

mother walking on a graded road (<u>here</u>), green plane of field

stretching toward where the wind would normally come from

fresh paint on floor, (<u>exact</u>) relation of its tone and color

to weight and mass of bricks across which the woman steps

rectangular shape of building surrounded by irregular curves

of a pastel tree, no sun above ridge after it rises (<u>one</u>)

(<u>not</u>) visible, the person whose remains include a coffee cup

with a chip on its rim and two lights on the pale dresser

6.13

curve of brown guitar in contrast to porcelain wall, feeling

(experience) of the absence in birds whether or not named

deer in yard, tip of branch where rose appeared (phenomenon)

which doesn't distract from the movement of missing color

old man at end of table turning something in his ear to hear

better, series of woman's earrings on opposite side (you)

(white) surfaces, windows and door trimmed in darker cypress

shade in relation to which it will therefore be connected

detail in landscape or the human event the word itself (how)

sounds, material for example of cloud film through window

6.14

black surface of table upon whose edge a pale (green) candle

sits, which doesn't matter in the larger scheme of things

looking out from where the wall is looking toward landscape,

(its) irregular curve of the grove through door's windows

bird's name above water, man on the right in black tee-shirt

who sees strong yellow light from the side ('experiment')

(could) be a summer dusk light above darker trees and ridge,

whiter grey as cloud unfolds between word and its feeling

sound of wall in relation to color of edge around it (order)

through which an image of the world happens, this in fact

126

6.15

moment the light first appears (<u>describe</u>), film below window

on green clumps of the field that isn't fog but a feeling

diving under as the approaching white wall of the wave hits,

(opposite) reaction of body to mass of object striking it

arriving after how many miles, low sounds of swells ("blue")

background to the also invisible trills of a song sparrow

man suddenly asking the older woman to marry him not knowing

the other woman struck by a tree, narrative pace (<u>effect</u>)

(<u>symptom</u>) of pain, sensation for example in back of left leg

collapsing when the man attempts to walk out of the water

6.16

sun coming up at almost farthest northern point, silhouetted

curves of the ridge between two stands of trees (<u>present</u>)

(<u>this</u>) connected to girl who stands in summer sunlight water

without moving, black of suit against white of a shoulder

green of lake's surface the foliage beyond reflects (<u>order</u>),

person leaning back against section of a worn wooden wall

something below the branch breaking the water's shaded plane

(<u>experience</u>), blond circle of head above it swimming back

sound of reading an echo of the shapes of letters themselves

shaped into words the reader will see, memory of (<u>theory</u>)

6.17

panorama of streets and buildings on hills in front of water

and more distant hills, words (<u>without</u>) meaning something

image (<u>where</u>) below spread-apart wings of large bird gliding

overhead, below which white half moon in blue morning sky

black enamelled body on top of other larger one still mating

(<u>define</u>) when the man walks back up cliff, ocean pounding

sun blinding the moment above the ridge not (<u>ever</u>) the same,

disappeared behind a wall of fog moving in from the south

music starting again, (<u>this</u>) view continued where wind bends

tops of hemlock and grasses in field against now grey sky

6.18

syntax of word meaning a reflection of world's syntax as man

'reads' it (<u>describe</u>), nasturtium orange on a green fence

grey-white of sky the fog inhabits, yellow of a petal fallen

on black surface of table in another room (<u>not</u>) now there

(<u>what</u>) next action off stage, woman reading a letter the man

presumably sent in response to something she perhaps said

analogy of sky in a picture to the actual fact of it outside

the window (<u>before</u>) more light enters, the bird next door

sounding off, (<u>function</u>) of the number in the same procedure

by which a person's hand passes from his head to the page

6.19

white of six roses in vase (possible) fading left of center,

speckled mass of granite propped against the window frame

line in liquid metal at edge of a copper ellipse, reflection

of the sun itself blinding a man at that angle (<u>indirect</u>)

(<u>not</u>) mirage of seeing, words for example detail of thinking

with something as it exists along a certain line of sound

grey-green wedge positioned on the right above which lighter

shades of a green infused with yellow, (<u>who</u>) thinks of it

feeling after (<u>it</u>) happens, birds missing a name in the dark

or cello whose notes echo the landscape of the man's body

6.20

palest of yellow petals around the still closed core, colors

of person's voice thinking what it reflects (<u>proposition</u>)

(<u>actual</u>) fact of things words could make be, fog above ridge

below which plane of field stretching far as the eye sees

loss of green staged in a fully orchestrated sound of events

(picture), theory punctuating moment's silence between it

man waking up from a dream in which person next to him turns

furrows over in garden rather than leaves, (<u>being</u>) called

title in parenthesis (<u>how</u>) music of word changes the viewer,

child in front row focused on father who reads toward him

132

6.21

birds up before first light (<u>spontaneous</u>) like sound itself,

which thereby enters the ear as the shape of words in air

deer in the yard (<u>thinking</u>) it, space filled by what happens

when a person hears that thing walking randomly toward it

yellow of building in middle distance on a green whose color

suggests a hill, (<u>this</u>) relation to feel of rose in glass

(<u>concept</u>) in fact, horizon perhaps of a pale band across top

above which blue and green compete for reader's attention

position of volume according to size and tone of its surface

in light of immediately contiguous surface, all or (<u>part</u>)

6.22

position of hand-shaped bowl whose glaze disappears in light

(optical), beside particular yellow of a just-picked rose

father's shy embrace of the mother after which, (that) child

at left of table who's dressed in black with two red lips

grey light on face like hair the man didn't forget to shave,

'marriage' for example not (always) a word but a sentence

irregular lower edge of grey-white sky on ridge, through two

panels of framed glass windows (seeing) feels isn't exact

same notes (completely) 'different,' where the cello follows

itself on a scale of intervals in terms of which is heard

6.23

abstract figure in the foreground (<u>causality</u>) next to second

action, person on sidewalk across the street hurrying off

yellow now more open, how (<u>that</u>) man at the microphone looks

like others in the black-with-red-ceiling mirror-lit room

place beside the window in which areas of lavender and green

suggest a landscape, a human form closing its eyes (<u>find</u>)

(<u>picture</u>) of person in lines of her chair, curve behind left

shoulder from which white of what frames the wall goes up

space around a flower imagined in terms of an opposite (<u>new</u>)

color, view through glass of stalk in water bent somewhat

6.24

angle (<u>reverse</u>) of yellow stretched to edge of page in book,

which is itself what everything exists to end up being in

dimension of time through the window measured by its opacity

of grey light between glass and ridge, thus (constructed)

(<u>not</u>) moving, how density of green leaves the space directly

in front of the viewer feeling something after sound hits

woman with white cup held against (<u>this</u>) blue form, pleasure

in the relative closeness or distance between such things

which color (<u>can</u>) occupy space, structure of an orange which

punctuates greens of a fence being one fact of perception

6.25

act of looking which becomes a dramatic event, (head) turned

toward the window where grey and white blankets the ridge

figure standing at middle center, stage directions including

how the word in a parenthesis will be changed (calculate)

(work) in terms of wall of sound before the person is awake,

how world of others in dream will be remembered if at all

yellow (one) below the now pale fact of a globe whose petals

haven't yet fallen, blue coming down through green leaves

girl on green blanket looking to her left, absence of (that)

feeling the man has when a note starts to play itself out

6.26

how all four globes fill the space around them, makes yellow

(solid) in relation to white wall or the greens beyond it

half of what's left of the man's face reflected in glass lit

from off-stage right (object), light at point of changing

paint on table flattened, feeling of blue below left of grey

volume of jar between which something else (real) happens

view of woman in color who is (not) far away, thin red dress

man being filmed in the room doesn't remember having seen

where she stops, green of lavender stalks framing right side

of plane on which yellow and orange may be this (applied)

6.27

(particular) grey where the fainter planet fades between two

others still visible, the space above the line of a ridge

grid of building framed by black of sky, to which an absence

(<u>there</u>) of light connects its mass to a surface behind it

darker blue of woman in chair beside a window (<u>not</u>) distant,

opposed for instance to circular shape of color in a bowl

orange (<u>picture</u>) in vase, curves of its vertical black lines

in contrast to greens of stems bent toward yellow on left

space within which the sound and/or motion of a bird happens

defined elsewhere, (<u>what</u>) thought itself imagines as this

6.28

so (<u>here</u>), how yellow in the background and a different tone

connect across the gap in which a building seems to exist

road going up from left to right against blue of sky, person

(<u>p</u>) speaking of second figure emerging from the landscape

scale of car apparently the same as one seen from that point

of view, a woman holding his head under her arm (concept)

(<u>straight</u>) angle of orange against the blue of water at edge

behind the man's back, which could be rotated 180 degrees

black and white rocks in the glass bowl imagined in relation

to great blue heron stalking across a field, (<u>this</u>) which

6.29

vertical columns of blue-green and blue (series) moving left

to right, angle of line from pearl below ear through eyes

(inside) his arm the girl facing the viewer, whose attention

interrupts the picture which is itself interrupted by him

repeating in fact, direction of music opposite feeling (one)

of notes perceived by the listener sitting in such a room

white walls beside green plane of the field, into whose grey

sound of a bird disappears before it enters (these) words

person (far) elsewhere, which leaves him thinking to himself

something missing from the corner between window and door

141

6.30

pattern of black bits on the windowsill where the faded rose

bends above them, (<u>this</u>) view beside grid of pastel roofs

(<u>where</u>) perspective changes, the body in shadow angled right

behind which light of blue-green surface breaking over it

how sun comes up not being noted (proof), clouds above ridge

opening a moment before an unknown bird or two disappears

plane of a picture seen on its side therefore being changed,

yellow of horizon extending vertically on right (example)

(<u>analysis</u>) of color itself 'read' as the sounds a bird makes

before the man opens his eyes to hear it, still not known

7.1

relation of white-orange on the edge of otherwise grey cloud

moving south above ridge, which is (<u>not</u>) in actual motion

note (<u>after</u>) notes in descending order, rhythm of whose word

follows what happens when the woman calls out of the blue

holding up a porcelain cup to her lips (<u>image</u>) for instance,

the feeling of not being next to the body thus missing it

sudden red of the man's jacket passing a window of the house

next door, after which the words themselves become (<u>real</u>)

(<u>calculation</u>) of color in field determined by viewer's place

in relation to this landscape, as a bird moves through it

7.2

thicket of branches the bird lands in (<u>between</u>) then leaves,

the person climbing up the ladder under and/or through it

consecutive weather, (<u>this</u>) figure in relation to the second

she calls as an impulse moves from left to right and back

not meaning actually to see him again, how different a sound

if tape changes direction or light 'shines' opaque (<u>side</u>)

(<u>part</u>) the song sparrow continues to play as landscape turns

from green to brown, dimension of a building in this view

house at intersection of a washed-out field of color (<u>form</u>),

vertical axis the distance between one person and another

7.3

greyish tint in the middle distance above green plane, (<u>not</u>)

space but absence of vertical textures beyond what's seen

yellow below band of pale blues to the right of actual color

of petals piled on a table, meaning picture changes (<u>one</u>)

(<u>it</u>) taking place off stage, the woman moving cup to her lip

elsewhere imagined as a syntax of suddenly related events

cars parked on street slanted upward to the right (<u>advance</u>),

feeling expressed as part of a word about to become sound

father holding the child (<u>if</u>) behind picture in which shapes

appear to be thought, first leaning back as another talks

7.4

almost all of yellow on the table below where the flower was

(that), woman's bare shoulder closer in light than before

(it) continued, view as a road climbs into fog of the figure

walking next to an image of the body she thought was gone

white wall seen in various shades of light (only), which one

thinks the other will be moving in the opposite direction

cello feeling the moment something pulls against its strings

followed by sound first of a bird then another, (picture)

which (that) one sees, wind beginning to move outside window

in leaves behind the woman holding up her coffee in a cup

7.5

grey-white outside window (<u>a</u>) through which a view continues

meaning itself, as a landscape becomes a series of sounds

bird for instance left of center point (<u>p</u>), where the person

at the table hears the sound an image leaves in its place

fallen yellow petals in a bowl, green wedge at top of a hill

above which the feeling of blue appears to be (<u>not</u>) there

how (<u>this</u>) happens in the time it takes these letters to get

into the left figure's ear, who thus becomes the listener

light circling down through the night sky accompanied by eye

who knows (<u>why</u>) something takes place, which is off stage

7.6

(how) color looks in different light, red roofs of buildings

to the left of which chimney against the neighbor's house

bodies in room watching images on wall (it) appears to echo,

something she feels coming toward this line at that angle

man on ladder for (example) sanding by hand, shape continued

moving forward and back in relation to the ridge above it

white between planes of glass through which the green leaves

(completely) still, as if events hadn't started to happen

before the woman in the car calls, man being loved by others

as the physical manifestation of an idea itself (more) so

7.7

dimensions of space in music as the second person leans back

(<u>thus</u>), the other figure whose hands gesticulate the beat

white walls in the next room, (<u>condition</u>) of red in relation

to its effect upon someone passing or walking in the gate

drop of water slipping from a leaf between the green foliage

in the window and the viewer who sees it, itself (<u>defined</u>)

(<u>this</u>), as the sound a black shape makes landing in the tree

following the letters in a bird's name as a crow flies by

tone's flat light after the person on the left calls (<u>form</u>),

door the color of sky itself reflected in a certain light

7.8

angle of hill disappearing into fog between lines (example),

the feeling of color in buildings moving as if in reverse

man at table hearing the woman walking across a wooden floor

who stops, (form) of pink open to white something he sees

(same) green in flat grey light, how in the car driving back

the sound that follows perception is like thinking itself

woman in the chair beside the window (proposition) opposite,

who in looking up catches an eye moving in that direction

one (that) changes, meaning of this action imagined in terms

of horizontal fields of color extending to plane of ridge

7.9

how (it) takes place in the space between leaves and the air

it touches moving it, darker foliage behind such an event

which word standing for off-stage action (<u>this</u>) for example,

the woman whose father dreams she has left without asking

subdued grey light, the balance itself visible in right hand

held at just the angle (<u>if</u>) one could have looked feeling

white door opening to absence of horizon the bird disappears

into for instance, which (<u>is</u>) also what a man first hears

(<u>that</u>) imagines anything as a series of related notes, green

vines grown under the roof below which light doesn't come

7.10

placement of leg in curve of other person's (_that_) isn't it,

where the action played on stage develops in visual terms

bird passing from right to left above the color of buildings

on opposite hill, the word for which isn't exactly (_this_)

(_these_) events assumed, first person turning in space of bed

imagined between the man's dream and next scene in street

woman whose eyes (_are_) therefore open, how the sound of wind

moving into the branches of a dark red tree isn't present

shapes in flat light through which the viewer's eye travels,

hands positioned on body adjacent to this (_other_) feeling

7.11

horizontal band across bottom of thought that (<u>is</u>) abstract,

whereas if sun climbs above the top of the ridge it isn't

reflection of man's face lit from the left beyond which wind

stirs leaves, sound of certain unknown birds (<u>imaginable</u>)

(<u>may</u>) be itself heard, acoustic phenomenon a memory of shape

of letters printed or drawn and/or the space between them

woman hearing in a man's voice something isolated (<u>counting</u>)

this distance from place to other place, where it happens

panorama of buildings on hill (<u>identity</u>) against the window,

in which feeling of depth becomes a two-dimensional field

7.12

(<u>knowledge</u>) the arrangement of color, shades of yellow ochre

in light which as it changes changes the perception of it

grid on paper (<u>interpret</u>), the person to whom it will appear

as landscape from the upstairs window above which nothing

allusions to the space behind figures whose eyes are closed,

(<u>philosophical</u>) in the sense that one does something else

scale above the table an image of how action happens between

a physical occurence and its sound, also (<u>related</u>) memory

echo (<u>posed</u>) as series of ascending notes, the woman the man

in another plane is watching suddenly also looking at him

7.13

blanket pulled off the woman's shoulder (language) which can

itself be seen, as letters sound an acoustic shape in air

two figures (expression) in the middle of a field whose path

appears to be moving, grasses in wind the water's surface

left side of house after light, same color around the corner

where the red plane below it reflects something up (<u>then</u>)

(<u>under</u>) top edge of cloud on ridge motion in black and white

panorama, man who sees this thinking anything is possible

woman touching him in that place which (<u>must</u>) have happened,

his memory of that feeling changing like colors on a wall

7.14

hummingbird stopped at the orange of nasturtium (phenomenon)

wanting to suck, another bird at window trying to get out

green frame around glass (action), second person in sunlight

moving toward the door which the first watching him feels

yellow of rose in the vase which doesn't mean something else

doesn't happen, (lack) of distance when he opens his eyes

(possible) thought, feeling color in woman's shoulder change

the vertical grey and white frame of the window beyond it

appearance of house from across the street continued in next

picture, in which the woman stands (anything) on his left

7.15

gold-lit (<u>of</u>) cloud above the horizon as the sun approaches,

after which curve of the ridge itself disappears in light

person seen from water level, whose reflection extends (<u>one</u>)

to the green foliage around it from which the other swims

apparently random arrangement of rocks placed on window sill

beside a glass object, (<u>these</u>) things not without feeling

(<u>circumstance</u>) in which the silhouette of a bird on a column

falls off, when what happens has its own particular sound

memory in place of (<u>that</u>) other place, in which other action

imagines how color fills up the shapes in a person's view

7.16

area beyond the irregular plane of the field (<u>given</u>) texture

by the weight of what's below it, which has nothing in it

memory of (<u>certain</u>) bird sounds through the half-shut window

before the man opens his eyes, thus another point of view

color around the house (<u>experiment</u>), as green becomes darker

light moving around to the street side of a white surface

dimension of vertical shapes in grid measured by its thought

(<u>under</u>) shade of neighbor's tree, such presence also felt

(<u>condition</u>) changed, wind above water's blue plane reflected

in the sound of a feeling through which something arrives

7.17

slow approach of light accompanied by the bird outside (<u>not</u>)

visible, feeling itself continued in a parallel direction

paler green of the eves, the man going up the ladder planted

against the background edge of the pink-white rose (body)

(<u>mechanical</u>) structure of field between viewer and the blank

missing, her being awake when the man moves away from her

like lavender in a glass (<u>how</u>) which sound penetrates, piano

for example not part of the present performance of action

parallel figures in vertical space observed from outside it,

(<u>both</u>) of whom might be mistaken from the person upstairs

7.18

addition of two parts black or something blue to green (<u>one</u>)

changing the way the subject looks in light, for instance

person in upstairs room standing as if she doesn't know what

she wants, whether to be continued elsewhere and/or (<u>not</u>)

(<u>a</u>) cup like a leaf, the woman holding the image to her lips

to the left of the otherwise grey-white space of a window

facing the grid of buildings on the opposite hill (example),

which isn't a memory but the sound of it in someone's ear

light behind irregular curve of trees in the middle distance

whose shape (<u>must</u>) be it, birds gliding by which isn't it

160

7.19

place where point (p) intersects the line between the inside

edge of a person's body and out, motion also part of this

sunlight on porcelain wall before she opens her eyes (here),

after which blue moving to grey as color like fog arrives

(not) there, leg's vertical position left of deep blue dress

falling against red of what seems to be a chair's cushion

frame of her walking past where the man on the ladder paints

area overhead, (method) by which green tint becomes black

which is (that) off stage action, sitting in a car elsewhere

not being stuck but unable to decide whether to drive off

7.20

half the shape of a bird's body (logic) which leaves pattern

of lighter shade in a green tree, grey sky where blue was

(mathematical), shift between the invisible sound in a field

another makes and the now almost black surface of a chair

earring on pillow after she sees him coming, (how) something

is parallel to a body of water thousands of birds land in

words inaudible as he crosses the membrane between (mention)

consciousness and sleep, meaning of such an action forgot

scale of right hand above the table in relation to white cup

in both hands next to it, both of whom glance off (logic)

7.21

bird's sudden sound from beyond the random shape of branches

in window, (situation) continued from some previous event

whose (consequence) doesn't matter, feeling of tobacco plant

leaves into which something passing casts a subdued light

weight of first color felt in terms of the next for example,

(a) vertical mass of pale green to the left of the center

building at far end of the sill, across from which landscape

descending from above an expanse of apparent space (more)

(and) still more action, faded yellow ochre wall in relation

to almost black green of frame and/or grey-white above it

7.22

planes of sound behind sound as the note fades, figure (<u>and</u>)

ground seen in motion from blue of shoulder to white wall

car's light broken (<u>so</u>), the man who follows it in film noir

to the place where the second woman is being held captive

(<u>this</u>) woman in cream-colored car repeated in the next scene

whose father becomes the other man, bird above grey field

street going up the hill, the shape on the left whose shadow

can be (<u>said</u>) to cover it when the picture is turned over

knife positioned in the man's nose (<u>act</u>) suddenly pulled out

which isn't remembered exactly, cloud not moving that way

7.23

window half-way closed, opposed to the two-dimensional image

whose reflection of the girl is a reading (<u>philosophical</u>)

(<u>essential</u>) color of walls depending on light and/or shadows

cast by body apparently lost in thought, observer implied

sound of dripping outside corner of house (<u>not</u>) visible, air

itself being an intangible presence descending from ridge

lavender in a glass on the table bending, memory (<u>different</u>)

of the woman whose face at that distance can also be felt

line between yellow (<u>logic</u>) of rectangular vertical building

and the orange above it, which had been in the other room

7.24

diagonal line of trees on ridge ascending to the right (<u>one</u>)

perception, followed by sound of water falling from eaves

man's left hand positioned on woman's left breast, half-full

glass in her left hand which may itself be imagined (<u>two</u>)

(point) at which the edge of the window intersects the chair

a possible focus, the other hand holding the cup's handle

motion of grass in wind an (<u>effect</u>) in space, invisible bird

which starts from the branch behind the viewer's shoulder

surface (<u>where</u>) its color stops, a line in which pale yellow

fills the air between this phenomenon and the wall itself

7.25

tobacco plant leaves to the right of the house (<u>calculation</u>)

in whose thickness an unknown bird appears, radio weather

(<u>same</u>) man at the window on aluminum ladder, body in a chair

standing for the figure in the bedroom who sees him there

meaning of rectangular area beyond the apparently invisible,

and/or shapes of more distant trees in contrast to (<u>this</u>)

(<u>concept</u>) following it, grey-green depth of water reflection

of the man breaking through the back of the breaking wave

arrangement of two-dimensional space itself (<u>also</u>) buildings

in color, foreground behind which more and larger of same

7.26

son too much in the sun (<u>physical</u>) in the first scene, blood

visible at his mother's mouth after she drinks from a cup

yellow of petal faded in bowl on table next to image of road

in shadow apparently going up hill, it also (<u>interpreted</u>)

(<u>it</u>) seems, green chair placed on bricks outside in relation

to an elbow on the curve of an arm in front of the window

something being inside such a place (<u>different</u>), her feeling

closer to the invisible sound his body against hers makes

action off stage including his appearance in her room (<u>this</u>)

after one person touches the ear of another, who's asleep

7.27

orange of nasturtium above the light green stem which stands

above branch of tree (possibility), wind moving in leaves

persistent sound of bird (one) invisible thing in other tree

followed by sight of second curving across window, corner

motion (that) shapes, whitish edge below grey texture of sky

into which a triangular portion of the ridge has vanished

scales below the angle of the woman's right forearm balanced

against background of wall, which is not itself (nothing)

(reflecting) this, how something leaves move as wind becomes

visible above the field whose stalks bend is also present

7.28

irregular curve of line at the top of the ridge itself (<u>not</u>)

this, below which the weight of it appears in first light

cloud body moving south in pale blue air, direction parallel

to what (<u>must</u>) be the edge of an otherwise invisible wind

shadows across the street climbing the hill on the left seen

from that position (<u>p</u>), backlit as sun's light approaches

(white) wall behind yellow, arrangement of rectangular grids

whose multiple feelings of color look something like this

lamp's globe reflected in glass (<u>now</u>), sound of which enters

line somewhere near the green frame of a different window

7.29

northwest 10 to 25 knots (<u>one</u>) acoustic event, space between

bamboo shoots plucked to penetrate the air which is music

profile of chair in window, weathered green against (<u>choose</u>)

random pattern of passion vine and/or nasturtium's orange

place in which (<u>nothing</u>) is but the shape of the sudden bird

moving overhead, in contrast to animal in wall not moving

color in relation to itself beside the first person singular

in front of an opposite window, woman in a blue dress (<u>B</u>)

(<u>surface</u>) texture, water in a glass vase turned the greenish

yellow of the stems submerged in it long enough to soften

7.30

looking out the same window every day, how a leaf moves once

drop falling from grey-washed sky hits it (<u>philosophical</u>)

thing that can't be described in words other than ones in it

(<u>proof</u>) of it, painting on table leaning against the sill

woman across from the first person who looks at her two eyes

looking back at him, which will happen in that (<u>position</u>)

(<u>this</u>) action also off stage, motion of tobacco plant leaves

in middle distance beyond which density of bamboo thicket

man on sidewalk holding the other man's hand a visual effect

(<u>something</u>), another man walking his dog toward the table

7.31

feeling absence of color (picture) above dark shape of ridge

which appears on the left, unknown planet faint as a star

echo of letters which (mean) shapes in air, a woman balanced

in front of the window through which nothing will be seen

black and white squares between which shades of grey (here),

how green or the light blue looks before an image arrives

silhouette of distant trees outlined against circle of still

invisible sun which comes up moments after it, (addition)

(interest) in that, action happening elsewhere being present

in the sound of something the man hears walking toward it

8.1

rose-colored flower out the window where nothing before was,

the hole in the ground into which roots planted (<u>subject</u>)

(<u>sense</u>) of animals under the house, pair of dogs for example

coming out to meet the person for whom nothing is changed

direction of second person moving toward a view of buildings

on the opposite hill (<u>mechanical</u>), his photograph of that

other off-stage (<u>action</u>) continued, including the way tulips

whose petals have fallen appear on table in adjacent room

swatch of white paint on shoulder of man's faded red jacket,

(<u>picture</u>) beyond it of how hills look painted above water

8.2

ball hanging from ceiling which as it turns reflects lights,

woman at the microphone reading (<u>movement</u>) of bee on road

wind out the window seen as the motion of plant (<u>p</u>), meaning

how something in the world becomes next or following word

position of man turning when the surface of water approaches

as a series of discernable marks above it, which is (<u>how</u>)

(<u>this</u>) will happen, woman with the balance in her right hand

below which string of something in light falling on table

other in chair facing the viewer (<u>without</u>) knowing it, brown

shoulder in relation to color of hand holding a white cup

8.3

silence of view a motion of leaves outside continues, (that)

itself becomes landscape light enters from off-stage left

misplacing the key somewhere between the reading and the car

parked upstairs, preceded by dislocation of finger (form)

(condition) of woman facing the source of light on the left,

letters whose shapes on a page change into something else

nothing beyond the green tops of branches in field but white

grey space (this) for example, building on hill in window

owl on bough (not) in car, the man standing behind the table

looking at a picture in which something glides diagonally

8.4

motion of bird in the green canopy of an unknown tree (<u>thus</u>)

seen, observer to whom the person has nothing else to say

(<u>same</u>) person hanging up the phone, meaning for the listener

registered the second time something begins to take place

sound outside the window (<u>thinking</u>) of an action which isn't

exactly there, words for different blues of air and water

whose feelings (surface), the woman in the room also in blue

reading a letter from someone who isn't therefore visible

sun finger's width above top of the ridge in (<u>this</u>) picture,

dragonfly's body stopped a moment in light's indifference

8.5

shape of bird flitting across glass of window from the right

which isn't the same as another, followed by contrast (x)

(that) doesn't happen off stage, his signature on the letter

before the man takes her hand not knowing what else to do

pair of other letters on the table whose meaning is (series)

spelled backwards, the oar which rows the small boat back

where the fact of things means only itself, which disappears

into the white fog above a field (it) in place of horizon

area of blue water parallel to miles of sand, lines of waves

breaking across longer distance than (before) this occurs

8.6

sunrise 6:17 (<u>that</u>) isn't seen, swell northwest 8 to 10 feet

after which a feeling of water moving in space takes over

pale green above blue-white square in grid whose colors echo

the sound of such shapes, depth of other sounds (<u>meaning</u>)

(<u>what</u>) a woman in blue thinks of it, about whom nothing else

of the subject who is also reading something can be known

motion of a leaf's surfaces in white frame's glass, (<u>single</u>)

person at edge of table holding a scale in her right hand

that something before it sounds like (<u>this</u>), two small girls

walking beside the mother whose relation can also be felt

8.7

view over left shoulder to the still wet surfaces of grasses

in field beyond the window, which happens in (<u>this</u>) order

woman's (gesture) walking toward car, hand lifted as the hat

tilts in wind that comes up from somewhere off-stage left

lighter brown patches on bird's wing as it flits from branch

(<u>picture</u>), figure moving through glass in house next door

man's hand in next scene placed on woman's left breast (<u>one</u>)

not seen, surface at that point rippled with yellow paint

cloud floating between the sunlit green of the field's grass

and irregular crest of ridge, above which blue (<u>possible</u>)

8.8

(<u>proof</u>) woman still in blue eyes closed, holding a white cup

to her lips whose shape the viewer must therefore imagine

where light begins to be felt outside (<u>now</u>) man's reflection

in glass, glass on wall whose blue-grey rim faces ceiling

clock in the dark inside of drawer the sound of which (<u>fact</u>)

matters, bird next door calling something through the air

vertical blue bar at the left of grid adjacent to suggestion

of window out which more, (<u>that</u>) this thought will follow

second (example) bird in motion against fog, beyond its grey

light the shape of something like trees also perhaps felt

8.9

top of empty green chair above which a dozen passion flowers

(physical) against fence, which isn't visible behind them

person reading a letter in front of the wall (_not_) that one,

first page on the table meaning the end of something else

flute followed by its sound (_image_), woman on couch in front

of whose reflection beyond which memory itself takes over

random drops of porcelain-white paint on glass for instance,

off-stage action including a building on a hill (_picture_)

(_this_) view continued, arms of dark trees in middle distance

moving against the still lighter hollow of space above it

8.10

man in a grey coat sitting with feet turned out (how) facing

the woman in a white dress, who's looking at someone else

six notes in descending order, (those) which echo the shapes

of feeling between the one who follows the one who leaves

person in car whose story isn't the same performed on stage,

music of event continued on viewer's left (demonstration)

(frame) of flowers behind her, the man picking up the letter

she threw to the floor thinking how sad it's come to this

absence of buildings on a hill, hummingbird at window moving

(situation) from entrance of pale pink flower to a branch

8.11

addition of green (<u>form</u>) continued on building, man thinking

back to where something might be said to have taken place

shape of color in left foreground also (<u>about</u>) space between

viewer and object perceived, who leans forward toward him

nothing blue visible above it, suggestion of where the ridge

stands in relation to (<u>see</u>) grey-white sky in front of it

woman holding white of cup in both hands for instance, man's

actions at this point not in fact her father's (<u>imagined</u>)

(<u>not</u>) in other words these terms, which blue or green colors

tobacco plant leaves in the window themselves approximate

184

8.12

nothing beyond what might be seen in (<u>this</u>) surface of white

clouds, the woman's action in not speaking equally opaque

sequence (<u>of</u>) events, where the figure standing at the table

reading a letter will also have said something to the man

color in painting on the wall in relation to porcelain-white

behind it, section of blue above like but not sky (<u>point</u>)

(<u>calculation</u>) of days approaching a thousand, how this woman

isn't present except as sound or shape of words in a line

bird moving through air (<u>a</u>) also sound the man hears walking

out the door, the same person not knowing what else to do

8.13

woman leaning forward in light in front of visual cue, map's

horizon directed to shape of the man's hat (<u>simultaneous</u>)

(<u>both</u>) at once thus stopping, his hand turned away from hers

who's already left thinking of what is or isn't occurring

worn places on front stairs of (<u>this</u>) house, woman elsewhere

waiting to return when the former person's car drives off

globe on the ceiling reflected in window through which sky's

grey begins to turn blue, but meaning something different

objects (<u>defined</u>) on dresser including a small bit of cloth,

woman in the shadows and the man's heart pinned to a wall

8.14

primrose petals turning to where light might appear (<u>that's</u>)

different from this, sound of six notes descending in ear

space between viewer and most distant building from the hill

above house whose windows face another direction, (<u>think</u>)

(<u>ambiguous</u>) action, woman in dark glasses opening a car door

before having decided whether or not she wants to do that

second man in a red jacket standing behind her at that point

(<u>perhaps</u>), coin in his right hand about to fall into hers

body of almost invisible tree through grey-white below which

vine on a fence (<u>structure</u>), back of an empty green chair

8.15

random motion of dozens of leaves and the grasses in a field

filling both windows, (<u>present</u>) feeling of moment passing

man leaving a message at woman's home (<u>condition</u>) elsewhere,

buildings on a grid of streets gradually slanting up hill

tone of her voice in his ear (<u>picture</u>) assuming he has asked

something about going on a walk, which isn't now possible

boy who hasn't changed, image of the woman holding the scale

in front of a window through which light enters (<u>process</u>)

(<u>thinking</u>) what happens after the man hangs up and walks out

the door, piano running first up then down the white keys

8.16

modulation of the grey scale out window (thought) continues,

water's surface through glass a feeling of depth below it

man at the older man's shoulder facing the viewer, something

about the position of the fingers in his right hand (<u>one</u>)

(<u>figure</u>) therefore present, relation of voices in other room

beyond which the sound of motion arriving at that instant

context meaning to include the relation between first person

sitting beside the window, (<u>position</u>) of second not known

silhouette of hummingbird stopping at edge of cypress (act),

where it lifts away leaving an empty place in the picture

8.17

light blue frame around (<u>language</u>) window of opposite house,

beyond which sound of train receding into middle distance

feeling of color in black and white (<u>note</u>), objects on floor

adjacent room whose shape exists in relation to other man

first man's position in front of the one who follows (<u>being</u>)

form of resentment, who chooses for example not to listen

green surface of water moving silence to the left of present

(<u>this</u>) moment, after which action continues in next scene

how (<u>that</u>) happens elsewhere, weight of man's body on ground

followed by perception and/or feeling of flat white walls

190

8.18

light through leaves of trees (knowledge) across the street,

direction a bird flies toward man measured in terms of it

action of body moving through room in relation to stationary

objects in it, which means that something happens (<u>point</u>)

(<u>p</u>) position of woman leaning toward the man who watches her

glass in one hand apparently lifting from it, for example

image previous to the person facing the viewer which (<u>means</u>)

something else, thinking that what takes place is visible

woman walking away from the car without looking back at him,

the man's impression (<u>somewhat</u>) colored by such a feeling

8.19

angle of door against wall before painting, whose (<u>movement</u>)

will shift depending on the pressure of left arm's stroke

room whose dimension seems from this perspective to increase

blue in place of land on a map, (<u>one</u>) person on the floor

man's hat in foreground beyond which (<u>what</u>) isn't said fills

the space between them, woman on right leaning toward him

appearance of first woman whose relation to man being struck

by the younger man includes a knowledge of that, (<u>single</u>)

(<u>pose</u>) to the left of the door, subject following a presence

as the sound of a distant car might be said to precede it

8.20

same arrangement of green leaves against grey of sky (<u>here</u>),

meaning the space betwen viewer and object hasn't changed

yellow of something like the building on a hill to the right

of which horizontal blue (<u>there</u>) is also sky, for example

woman on phone looking at foreground, man in different place

having returned by car to hear something about it (<u>sense</u>)

(<u>under</u>) lower corner of map the back of an empty blue chair,

profile of head tilted toward the letter held at its edge

nothing beyond green of passion vines on a fence except more

grey against ridge, (<u>one</u>) note after another in next room

8.21

yellow of rose petals above (surface) of table, its relation

to vertical yellow column of building on left approximate

woman on phone also not present in that case, where thinking

of her moving about another room is possible (assumption)

(being) itself, concluding what happens after certain action

takes place in the grey above the field beyond that fence

something for instance falling from sky in (another) window,

glimpse of brown tobacco plant leaf on left about to fall

sound of the man's shoulder when she pushes it back that way

(same) as motion, left side of body also therefore normal

8.22

wedge of blue-grey something on wall of white room (<u>itself</u>),

person waking to the sound of how to pronounce the island

still not fallen, density of petals behind whose pale weight

arrangement of color in a grid meaning nothing but (<u>what</u>)

(<u>this</u>) event including a suggestion of purple flower on left

followed by angle of hand on white cup, blue of the dress

window facing nothing but the grey above parallel (<u>position</u>)

surface of a green field, woman's voice in the other room

second person at water's edge (<u>blank</u>), from where he watches

seeing her starting to move suddenly in another direction

8.23

blue which appears, (<u>angle</u>) of sun's approach above suddenly

visible ridge whose image frames the field in front of it

landscape below water moved to the left of the screen (<u>one</u>),

woman surrounded by foliage reaching toward reddish-black

direction a bird turns without thinking, place of this sound

in the picture colored by the feel of light (<u>calculation</u>)

(<u>therefore</u>) motion of leaf in wind, green and/or light brown

looking through the window toward action which isn't seen

second person bending to her left at the waist for instance,

(<u>these</u>) events happening in the time it takes to say them

8.24

sense of pale yellow (<u>abstract</u>) green at lowest right corner

of window, beyond which darker green of vine left of gate

rose also in foreground, how the face of the woman (imagine)

behind its leaves shifts as viewer's head moves before it

motion of grass in grey distance of otherwise invisible air,

notes whose feeling seems to echo these events (<u>opposite</u>)

(dimension) of present action for example, man unable to eat

something about the place of red which enters the picture

eye's diagonal from lower left to upper right edge (<u>systems</u>)

of color, back turned between seated and standing figures

8.25

rectangular arrangement to the right (<u>of</u>) left window, frame

in which a bird turns suddenly into the following picture

head looking over left shoulder, the woman's half-open mouth

level with the earring hanging from her left ear (<u>series</u>)

(<u>such</u>) as these notes, music in the other room whose feeling

seems to echo the shape of something air and/or ear hears

sound of water surrounding the body dropping into it, (<u>form</u>)

of grey-green depending on the reflection of sky above it

yellow (<u>concept</u>) below edge of the opposite vertical window,

appearance including motion of branches across the street

8.26

stack of three rocks centered on marble table, couple (<u>this</u>)

to closed windows out which a feeling of grey-green scene

second person between two others facing viewer's (direction)

whose head turns, an echo of the sound of her white dress

image of woman looking in through glass, (<u>calculus</u>) of color

implied in the grey scale of a leaf in front of her waist

man waking in middle of night also thinking this, how clouds

move against suggestion of ridge beyond in next (<u>picture</u>)

(<u>a</u>) diagonal of left foot placed in relation to the person's

on her right, whose angle itself seems pointed toward his

199

8.27

petal in corner of eye (one) falling, palest yellow on right

edge of shape of others which have landed there before it

reflection in window's surface, where ('x') equals the man's

experience of being in that place looking at what happens

which isn't a (question), three figures on a bench the first

of whose arm reaches casually behind the woman's shoulder

grey light above the field before the sun rises behind ridge

which won't at that point be seen, presence of blue (not)

(spatial) configuration of notes in air, where one's feeling

of something which happens elsewhere continues to echo it

8.28

horizon level with the upper edge of first woman's (glance),

shadow of man's head projected on face of rock below left

also in blue standing (after) looking at letter to the right

of the table, the visual shape of its sound enclosing her

image for instance in the middle distance, profile of a bird

to the left of her shoulder apparently facing him too (a)

(variable) assumed motion of waves, whose darkest blue faces

approach as if from behind the center of what's happening

random arrangement of yellow blossoms (b) on plane of table,

her right hand balanced on the tilted surface of the rock

8.29

tobacco plant leaf hanging by a thread beyond (logic), glass

through which feeling travels close to the speed of sound

also looking back over left shoulder, note on back (<u>example</u>)

an image the hand leaves of something on the yellow plane

space behind the blue of water where a pale grey-white field

is crossed by a horizontal line, who isn't present (<u>that</u>)

(<u>this</u>) continues as an action, the woman walking into a room

holding the dark-haired infant the man isn't a witness to

no view beyond what's possibly seen there, (<u>how</u>) the silence

in the other room follows what takes place in front of it

8.30

yellow ochre in the distance (picture) of the upper surface,

below which an after-image of the action which disappears

relation between the man on the left holding a glass of wine

and the girl in white leaning toward her mother, (<u>define</u>)

(<u>grammatical</u>) identity, contour of landscape in the distance

of the table by the window listening to its physical echo

interval after which it sounds again, the woman's (<u>decision</u>)

to look toward him not meaning what she feels can be seen

place below clouds light appears to happen, (<u>how</u>) this event

moves a branch in the air where nothing seems to touch it

8.31

reflection of ceiling in window on left opposite (structure)

half-full glass on wall, distance measured from the floor

woman in black and white (concept) whose feeling isn't seen,

the meaning of absence for instance before the man enters

scale of figures in relation to grid on the floor the second

of whom turns away, man speaking to her with (conviction)

(empirical) perception of color, orange nasturtium on a wall

bird in motion suddenly stops a moment or two in front of

sound of the woman's voice (first) noted, grey-white in left

corner seeming to push against the surface from inside it

9.1

space beyond the person reflected in plane of glass imagined

as distance between it and what's not visible, (position)

(first) that sound recedes into a silence, light brown wings

on a white sill against which its shape becomes a feeling

air above the water's surface as person (p) slips out of it,

circular pattern of something in the dark moving under it

shape and/or color of the second letter (imaginable) subject

to this, profile of woman in blue holding it in left hand

continuous unfolding of previous event, (logic) for instance

of person on left looking back at the man who watches her

9.2

outline of branch suspended in air, where the sound (<u>system</u>)

the man sitting in front of it hears happens on the right

head bent for example, tobacco plants in the middle distance

a singular feeling of loss in that position (co-ordinate)

(<u>x</u>) perhaps something the emotion his letter to her implies,

which she internalizes driving in the green car elsewhere

yellow of petals falling in bowl, grey and/or white (<u>series</u>)

both sides of and behind the woman who apparently sees it

thinking the shape of the small bird crouched in the doorway

isn't exactly the same thing as it, (<u>calculus</u>) of a color

9.3

center of window above the girl in a white dress (<u>different</u>)

looking at something in her lap, feeling distance of that

light behind arrangement of leaves ('<u>a</u>'), rectangular events

positioned in such a grid according to color and/or shape

woman at table looking over the yellow of her left shoulder,

space between her thinking of him and the wall (<u>measured</u>)

(<u>calculation</u>) for instance, how shades of green above viewer

seem to follow the invisible sound a bird makes behind it

person ('<u>x</u>') in relation to her, the position of a white cup

in front of a mouth which isn't therefore exactly present

9.4

words taking color from the world, which continues (forward)

to the part about the woman running up to him in the dark

greenish-white blossom hanging from nothing below the branch

(<u>imagine</u>), random motion following what appears to happen

second person not knowing what feeling it is, as if presence

changes something between the rocks on the table (<u>result</u>)

(<u>several</u>) feet to the right of it, blue of the woman's shoes

seen at oblique angle to the left of the man's black ones

bone turned on its side below the center of the left window,

(<u>calculus</u>) of the three-dimensional figure relative to it

9.5

pinkish edges of grey-white clouds above darker shape (<u>that</u>)

becomes the ridge, which as viewer looks again turn white

cylindrical bodies centered against the feeling of colorless

sky, whose two-dimensional thinking seems to stop (<u>there</u>)

(<u>what</u>) takes place off stage, the woman at a table returning

to what his letter must have said about a previous action

circles of sound inside of which a bird appears to be closer

than water, (<u>possible</u>) notes whose feeling fills the room

paler green horizon across the top of a black and white grid

of which nothing else is known, (<u>condition</u>) which appears

9.6

curve where cloud appears to descend in a shape like (<u>this</u>),

below which hummingbird perched on the branch on the left

figure at the edge of the blue-green wave moving as it moves

(phenomenon), color at that moment perceived as its sound

space beyond vines which cover the fence farther than viewer

thought possible, (<u>calculation</u>) of the distance behind it

arrangement of color rotated on its side, a horizontal image

changing to the window a small bird hits in black (<u>white</u>)

(<u>how</u>) something looks, position of the girl closer to mother

than person on her left whose left arm reaches behind her

9.7

blue-white disk framed below branches in the west ("green"),

which as light increases falls deeper into negative space

angle of man's right hand brought toward her right shoulder,

(<u>its</u>) relation to what isn't seen in front of her unknown

water's surface (psychological), that feeling of being in it

continues the direction away from the absent first person

vertical position of a leaf about to fall, language of white

clouds above top of the ridge whose meaning isn't (<u>clear</u>)

(<u>order</u>) in thinking, as something happens in the first place

without quite knowing what its color and/or shape will be

9.8

surface of landscape from the hill (<u>describe</u>) in front of it

reversed in the scale outside it, edge of door not closed

chair's curve to the left of the window facing it (opposite)

the observer, feeling of space between hand and white cup

looking over a left shoulder, the angle of the woman's mouth

which implies color of previous and present events (<u>blue</u>)

(<u>effect</u>) of yellow also felt by the man who sees it, shadows

across the hill from building on left perpendicular to it

sound of second bird (<u>that</u>) is starting to answer the first,

another motion above the top of the field possibly not it

9.9

something like wind (<u>present</u>) but not, which is how it looks

before light comes into the room from a source outside it

grey and/or bright white above horizontal dimension of ridge

moving away from him, feeling subject to man's (<u>position</u>)

(<u>order</u>) of adjacent colors for instance, green beside yellow

surfaces of petals in a glass after which nothing happens

body passing first to the right across a field (<u>experience</u>),

sound from opposite corner of what a bird itself might be

motion of tallest grasses not (<u>mechanical</u>), edge of branches

which seem to project the interior of thinking outside it

9.10

first light behind the corner casting image of tree's branch

against it, the outline of which doesn't (<u>mean</u>) something

feeling (<u>where</u>) it happens, how the man doesn't exactly know

what words follow him inside the physical envelope of air

layers in which the person listening hears (<u>some</u>) bird, what

takes place beyond it continued in paler blue above ridge

standing between two empty chairs, figure reading the letter

(<u>more</u>) whose silence will suddenly start to fill the room

edges moving as if through glass, (<u>this</u>) green leaf opposite

the woman who sees him stopping in front of the white car

9.11

vertical edge of window against which light (<u>describe</u>) hits,

grey-white expanse of ridge filling in space to the right

where the man's right hand is placed, her face in the mirror

glancing at the subject he imagines she doesn't see (<u>not</u>)

(<u>immediate</u>) sense of it, shape of a bird for example outside

the sound it makes before the man actually opens his eyes

light reflected on surface of pool also (<u>before</u>) it happens,

followed by the feeling of the left leg floating below it

back of her shoulders beyond which letters she faces on wall

in front of her (<u>function</u>), which therefore can't be seen

9.12

sound of owl itself (position) hooing from tree in the dark,

the three-note ascending sequence from the bird next door

coming up over shoulder of the ridge, sun's light (multiply)

which floods the picture with something that wasn't there

beyond where edge of slope on the right intersects the other

going up, appearance of water's white shot into air (not)

(who) can't see a thing, blackness of ground below left foot

punctuated by millions of small white lights moving in it

how (it) takes place, person below surface of water swimming

through it toward feeling of lighter green area around it

9.13

bright yellow edge of the building to the left of sky's blue

(<u>content</u>) outside, analogous to the paler color beyond it

relation between the shape of letters (<u>actual</u>) and the woman

looking over her shoulder, whose feeling fills that space

bird moving in middle distance above the field which becomes

its silence, followed by notes' ascent in next (<u>position</u>)

(<u>being</u>) man's face in the upper right corner, hers continued

in front of the painting of coming back to present moment

blue surfaces divided by (<u>series</u>) perpendicular black lines,

horizontal yellow above it adjacent to petals it imagines

9.14

drop of water about to fall from tip of leaf's (<u>spontaneous</u>)

green, beyond thicket of bamboo through which light comes

grey rectangular field on the white wall, window on the left

(<u>concept</u>) an emptiness of fog above plane analogous to it

colors in a grid turned on its side in relation to something

the man sees from the water's surface, which isn't (<u>this</u>)

(<u>one</u>) possibility, the woman's feeling compared to a picture

and/or the sound it makes approaching from off-stage left

letter positioned at lower left edge of the map for example,

whose texture appears to be (<u>part</u>) of what she's thinking

9.15

angle of person's left arm slanted toward reflection of face

(optical), end of first event become the start of another

darker shape at the far edge of the field, spaces between it

and what isn't seen beyond it measured in terms of (that)

(is) itself something, the woman holding the cup to her lips

which therefore aren't visible to the person opposite her

glimpse of the bird behind the man's right shoulder (seeing)

the moment before its sound is heard, precedence of notes

orange of second flower (pulling) the same orange toward it,

where wall of house meets green of foliage surrounding it

9.16

not green but the atmosphere between leaves and the observer

(sense) through which it passes, before its sound arrives

face in background of clouds in sky, numbers in right corner

compared to his feeling (<u>calculation</u>) which can't be seen

first the bird on a bare branch in a field (<u>find</u>) then gone,

action thus happening in the time it takes to perceive it

yellow ochre across top of the plane beyond which pale green

road curves up hill to the right, trees on left (<u>picture</u>)

(<u>picture</u>) in window of what's outside it, second bird moving

the structure of leaves when it leaves its position there

9.17

horizontal strip of grey-white fog moving below top of ridge

(<u>reversed</u>) edge of field in the distance, that is feeling

figure on right in blue (<u>one</u>) reaching toward second person,

the finger of whose right hand appears to be receiving it

light itself, which transcribes an object's exterior surface

repeated as a bird rises not moving except as sound (<u>not</u>)

(<u>this</u>) green in relation to actual density of cypress branch

behind a white door, ambient sound in back of that action

man's feeling implied as such (<u>assertion</u>), thought of bird's

yellow against the pavement above which the person passes

9.18

close-up of man's mouth opening (<u>meaning</u>) the sound he makes

isn't heard, her face in glass watching over his shoulder

which before yellow, arrangement of petals on a table beside

the green cup disconnected to its former condition (<u>over</u>)

(<u>sphere</u>) half present above the cobalt of a sky it imagines,

figure in the background bending to pick what she sees up

film of clouds passing to the right framed by window, (<u>less</u>)

visible when light appears over the shoulder of the ridge

eyes closed, the woman in a chair on the left in second view

(theory) thinking something inside the blue-green surface

9.19

presence of the invisible vertical plane (<u>solid</u>), atmosphere

beginning to imagine the feeling of where blue itself was

thinking, man at the table across from the second person (<u>a</u>)

surface of the landscape at water level looking toward it

sound before light enters, which isn't the same as something

appears to be driving in the dark away from it (distance)

(<u>not</u>) image of figure on left in opposite corner of the room

for instance, how the woman opens the door following that

texture of air (<u>applied</u>) to body, through which sound itself

moving out from the center of an event seems to disappear

9.20

allusion to color in right corner, blue and/or green feeling

(particular) to the lower half of the window for instance

birds lined on a telephone wire which isn't exactly (there),

something about the sound of invisible traffic through it

wall of the adjacent room blank beyond the dark of the plant

beside the glass door, off-stage action (not) seen by her

following the previous scene, person reading letter in light

not of what happens but arriving from left side (picture)

(that) isn't equal to spatial dimension through which a bird

descends, as thought into which something also disappears

9.21

yellow-orange globe at mouth of a glass (here) sound passes,

the grey-white feeling of air surrounding it for instance

woman closing the door upstairs, infant in man's lap staring

at the intersection of two vertical planes (p) of counter

second ('number') person leaning over something on page held

at lower left corner of map, distinct blue of the surface

density of a field corresponding to the texture of emptiness

over it, through which the speck of the bird turns (away)

(this) same picture not repeated exactly, woman in the chair

behind whom pale yellow of rectangular building on a hill

9.22

facing the observer, head perpendicular to angle of left arm

reaching in front of a wall against which corner (series)

(<u>inside</u>) light reflected in window's otherwise black facade,

man at the table therefore thinking in the opposite logic

grid for example blue and/or green squares in relation (<u>one</u>)

to black and white image above it, as feeling also leaves

action itself in (<u>fact</u>), where something happening elsewhere

isn't noticed except as light on the surface of the ridge

person's voice to the left of following sound (<u>how</u>) missing,

exterior view of object suggesting his feeling toward her

9.23

second scene in (this) order, transparent shape on the right

corresponding to color and/or feeling of woman next to it

orange above yellow of the body centered (where) it happens,

man moving toward the two-dimensional chair on the screen

whiteness of vase at edge of the table above which something

(picture) doesn't exist, two hands clasped in back of him

present action as word passes through it toward body on left

moving in time to echo its music, which isn't (different)

(that) is to say also present, the person reading the letter

standing by herself at the table in a different situation

9.24

diagonal line of shadow on white wall behind the man (<u>looks</u>)

like this, light above the shape of leaves through window

place an unknown bird lands a moment before the body leaves,

where sound follows the act of seeing itself passing (<u>it</u>)

(<u>cut</u>) through weight of air, density of water whose surfaces

reflect the motion of a cloud above person immersed in it

disappearance of speaking subject to area at far side (<u>real</u>)

landscape, the field beyond which vertical plane of ridge

interior feeling of blue square in right corner for instance

(<u>calculation</u>), man then walking away from her in the dark

9.25

view from which motion changes leaves through window's glass

(<u>between</u>) where bird lands and grey above it, for example

black and white grid of rectangular blue or green (<u>x</u>) shapes

not identical, as feeling below body's surface takes over

place where notes start to go up, followed by the appearance

(<u>equation</u>) woman at table registered as light on left arm

drop falling from edge of tobacco plant leaf before opposite

direction of her thinking, green extending outward (<u>from</u>)

(<u>form</u>) of reflection in mirror watching him, detail of man's

half-open mouth suggesting something the viewer can't see

9.26

leaves below roof of adjacent house moving (concept) in wind

and the sound it makes, illegible scrawl driving in a car

perpendicular to line above blue field in lower right corner

(one), person sitting beside the other thinking something

across the space between two chairs, or else leaning forward

where words in the air themselves become the feeling (it)

(in) reverse direction of a bird appearing on branch outside

center of three vertical windows, blond braid pulled back

body settled below the surface of water in the dark (logic),

blue-green tone of sky around a pair of trees on the left

9.27

half the yellow petals fallen on table left of woman in blue

holding white cup to her lips, (how) other sounds outside

across from the girl in the car saying something about (it),

man beside her hearing the picture of what he doesn't see

direction of bird moving from right to left across top third

image in window glass (only) after it's gone, for example

person spinning away from someone on left to man beside her,

the feeling behind the skin that's seen being seen (what)

(that) is meaning itself, the present condition of an object

when a bird lands on a green chair and/or then disappears

9.28

place where color stops (<u>a</u>) next to the figure at the table,

angle of arm held above it in relation to silence in room

shaft of light slanting down through sky, as feeling mirrors

grey-white surface of water across which wind isn't (<u>that</u>)

(<u>not</u>) first person approaching thought of pale yellow petals

previous to intersection of cloud and ridge, sky above it

notes which ascend in the next room, (<u>this</u>) feeling of sound

perceived behind the man's face in the upper right corner

following action, orange something exposed in opening clouds

and/or opposite the window of blue car which (<u>must</u>) be it

9.29

line between spaces before it and after (<u>this</u>) for instance,

edge of a branch in grey sky reflected in water's surface

texture of the vertical plane of the ridge, (<u>how</u>) it happens

prior to the sound of an invisible bird in tree behind it

shape of the leaf between the edge of one plane and the next

which intersects a rectangular building, whose (position)

(<u>calculate</u>) relation between the man writing it at the table

and the woman standing elsewhere, choosing not to respond

man leaning into space of the feeling which separates (<u>more</u>)

him from her, whose profile appears in the adjacent plane

9.30

disappearance of bird in flight curving below edge of window

(<u>now</u>) up to chair's back, other sound following elsewhere

objects on table in negative space, a magnification of lines

parallel to the side of water framed in glass (<u>condition</u>)

(<u>defined</u>) in terms of action happening prior to thinking it,

the woman sitting in that position before traffic arrives

motion of leaf after it falls (gone), notes in the next room

echoed in the distance between edge and the air it leaves

invisible feeling inside a person moving to the door, (<u>form</u>)

something passes to the right of the window looking at it

10.1

feeling of motion in green plane beyond still closer greens,

after which the music starts the first movement (example)

(different) situation, man standing beside the door when she

walks in and kisses him first on one cheek then the other

five-note descending series followed by blank, (description)

opacity of grey-white area above the surface of the field

thought of the body inside (<u>this</u>) thought, the woman sitting

to the left of an interior window open in relation to her

person also on the left beginning to speak (<u>one</u>) what sounds

like her voice, whereas something didn't happen like that

10.2

smallest of blue rectangular shapes (concept), which thought

visible as the body moving between sky and plane of field

lower part of man's body plainly visible below chair, (this)

space in relation to wall against which woman is standing

looking over left shoulder toward an interior view described

as a pattern of black and white squares, which it (isn't)

(that) perception for instance, the way a leaf moves exactly

through glass in the distance between it and the observer

opening of a cloud (next) to the blue above it, crow's sound

behind the position of branches it lands in and/or leaves

10.3

shapes on line of ridge (extension) behind which sun appears

out of distance, which before wasn't something to be felt

interval between the moment it leaves and orange-pink clouds

above the horizon, spaces thereby transformed (calculate)

(these) events prior to memory of an action, woman rereading

the letter by the table written by the person it imagines

emotion of various greens in foliage (without) which nothing

will be changed, the "f" at the end of "of" become an "r"

absence of viewer, (other) person in the mirror for instance

glancing to the left over her right shoulder toward floor

10.4

blue an approaching cloud (<u>could</u>) be changed into, sculpture

erasing the line imagined between the painting and itself

girl walking beside the man not looking at him (<u>imaginable</u>),

the woman in a different location still thinking about it

relation of grey to white feathers on a bird's breast framed

on a branch in the window (<u>a</u>), isn't the same thing as it

vertical yellow column on left edge against planes of leaves

corresponding to idea of flower in foreground, (<u>counting</u>)

(<u>identity</u>) of color itself, dimension continuous as the wind

above the field moves from elsewhere to feeling it appear

10.5

light as bird moves from its first appearance to (<u>knowledge</u>)

of it, beyond which particles also of light drifting away

position of moon in relation to brightest planet, the person

who's looking up from beneath water's surface (<u>interpret</u>)

(<u>investigation</u>) of that including what takes place off stage

before she arrives, approaching to touch him on the cheek

horizontal view of buildings (<u>related</u>) by green and/or blue,

color in the first place but not exactly in control of it

interrupted by sound of man coming in, who places the pillow

(<u>purpose</u>) across the opening of the second person's mouth

10.6

interchange of state (psychological) as pink-orange of cloud

becomes a grey-white feeling, and/or idea analogous to it

sound (figure) system, distance of the bird outside the door

measured by the time it takes an acoustic image to arrive

man turning back to the person who calls across such a space

(then), opposite her response to the surface of an object

addition of yellow element in plane between viewer and glass

whose meaning will therefore be transparent, (understood)

(not) random order of events but the shape of it, perception

in which a small bird disappears into green at the corner

10.7

element in the exterior of the composition changed by motion

as wind surrounds the edges of green leaves, (phenomenon)

(gestures) toward the second person, whose perception of him

continues as an experience of an event in relation to her

moon's light in negative space between (position) buildings,

compared to how another action might take place by itself

silence of an object (possible) after the note stops, a form

of the body submerged in water which floats and dissolves

following (anything) observed from a different point of view

for instance, performance interrupted when she walks away

10.8

thought of yellow (<u>qua</u>) yellow in picture of petals on table

below actual color, where the two-dimensional frame stops

space outside the window's plane, which extends beyond (<u>one</u>)

what the viewer sees looking not at but through its glass

curve of feeling between face turned back over left shoulder

and the ground behind it, and/or relation between (<u>these</u>)

(<u>circumstances</u>) by which the man enters the water head-first

approaching condition of object, surface opposed to depth

actual green of "leaves" in relation to hearing (<u>this</u>) sound

of leaf, what takes place between seeing and/or saying it

10.9

vertical arrangement of cars parked along the side of a hill

adjacent to shadows (<u>position</u>) of buildings, for instance

descending sequence of three notes, which enters the picture

as sound in the window above the empty bed (<u>mathematical</u>)

(<u>proof</u>) another bird approaching the left side of the house,

slant of light through half-open door behind the observer

head turning half toward the person standing on left (<u>under</u>)

circle in corner of map, yellow ochre of book at shoulder

distance between feeling of (<u>what</u>) happens and its condition

where horizontal plane of field intersects ridge, example

10.10

absence of detail (<u>both</u>) in and on surface of object, person

not constructing the idea of what happened in terms of it

otherwise invisible wind in leaves (<u>not</u>) previously noticed,

in whose various green shades light itself is transformed

grey-white texture of field in lower left corner in relation

to vacant space in window behind her, shape of her (body)

(<u>mechanical</u>) feeling of the white porcelain cup in left hand

for example, the orange of nasturtium hanging from branch

picture of color in window adjacent to transparency of glass

behind it, (<u>how</u>) object changes in a second person's view

10.11

membrane between things outside window (<u>one</u>) and/or on table

dissolved, feeling itself moved to interior point of view

hand across left shoulder in the night, afterimage appearing

to be the color between the wave and sound it makes (<u>not</u>)

(<u>a</u>) absence of the person prior to experience of actual legs

for example, three-note descending call of bird on branch

off-stage action seen (<u>via</u>) language, woman whose white face

doesn't change the way the motion of both her hands might

lateral direction of two small birds in flight (<u>one</u>) against

pale blue above the line of the ridge, therefore extended

10.12

pale yellow globe beside orange of closed poppies (<u>analysis</u>)

in a glass, color of an image becoming the shape of sound

subject in the greyish-white plane above curvature of field,

the person on the left turning toward the observer (here)

(<u>not</u>) like thinking but being in it, horizontal axis implied

in the perception of waves arriving across great distance

disappearance of the first person (<u>mathematical</u>) in relation

to woman in blue reading a letter, whose feeling isn't it

grey car stopped in traffic at corner (<u>there</u>), parallel blue

below darker blue square above it and/or edge on the left

10.13

two-toned pitch of an invisible bird behind the viewer, echo

of color in the surface of a picture where meanings (<u>are</u>)

(<u>here</u>), yellow shape of the building in the window analogous

to feeling a physical column of light coming down on left

slippage between an exterior situation and looking out at it

from the inside, (<u>how</u>) the woman's head tilts to the side

sun possibly also visible (<u>mention</u>), sound of plane overhead

when the jay lands on the horizontal arm of a green chair

absence of a color in upper right corner (<u>position</u>) opposite

light blue square, thought of which takes place before it

10.14

black shape on a bare branch followed by crow's (<u>situation</u>),

where the meaning of its sound becomes a form of thinking

black and white close-up of the woman's face shot from above

which action stops, man who approaches the bed (<u>sequence</u>)

(<u>mathematical</u>) relation between feeling and absence of color

for example, white clouds moving against pale blue ground

bird in motion (<u>appearing</u>) behind the viewer, half-open door

out which the sound of its landing or leaving isn't heard

outline of leaves defined by (<u>logic</u>) presence of light above

elsewhere, wind moving the condition of object in field

10.15

dimension in which the sound of a bird (<u>and</u>) meaning happens

simultaneously, one parallel to another for instance here

figure on the right reaching out her hand (<u>so</u>), the man also

watching her from his position at edge of left foreground

grey light above irregular top of ridge in relation to faded

yellow rectangle, and/or condition of not thinking (<u>this</u>)

(<u>said</u>) in green car when the phone stops, the person hearing

something repeated about the structure of previous events

motion of taking off from a branch (<u>act</u>) remembered in words

other than it, color of a rose in a glass to be continued

10.16

body beneath the water's surface moving toward idea of plane

(<u>philosophical</u>), the space of the sky where the stars are

five-note descending sequence after (<u>this</u>) for instance, how

feeling of a bird's sound echoes its position on a branch

woman in blue whose back turns to the window (<u>not</u>) watching,

opposite girl whose lips feel the coldness of man's cheek

following example of yellow scattered on table, song sparrow

stopped in light at the edge of a pine branch (<u>different</u>)

(<u>logic</u>) of next situation, which includes the motion of head

hummingbird plunges into the orange mouth of a nasturtium

10.17

shadows of branches on the fence (<u>one</u>) in a different place,

observation of the molecule which in theory doesn't exist

position of ladder against house in relation to wall's color

and/or its feeling in a certain light, which isn't (<u>that</u>)

(opposite) thought of distance, what takes place between man

on the phone and the one who doesn't answer not explained

shape of black dog on the side of the road imagined (<u>effect</u>)

of saying it, preceded by walking elsewhere not seeing it

membrane wrapped around corner of a building whose dimension

will thus be changed, (<u>where</u>) the wall itself isn't white

10.18

white moving in a pattern faster than thought itself, random

(<u>calculation</u>) of adjacent notes included in the first one

other bird landing in (<u>same</u>) tree, sound in repeated section

which is therefore not identical in its second appearance

for example, variation in the feeling of a note whose motion

continues as an event which happens to the left of (<u>this</u>)

(<u>concept</u>) of color curved around body of clouds, where green

becomes an appearance of the visible shape being observed

horizontal plane across which the feeling of water is (<u>also</u>)

echoed, which the imagination of the sound isn't thinking

10.19

opposite wall in white room not exactly described (<u>physical</u>)

in terms of its appearance, a person walking out the door

action for example repeated here, feeling of pale blue plane

rising from behind a pattern of green foliage (<u>interpret</u>)

(<u>it</u>) in relation to the surface of the woman turning in bed,

something about the sound of thinking coming down on left

angle as if looking through (<u>different</u>) window, glass itself

subject to a perception of event which doesn't take place

distance between the position of man's left shoulder and arm

in (<u>this</u>) instance, the echo of another part of her shape

10.20

image of second person's thought (<u>possibility</u>) at the table,

an interior emotion reflected in glass looking back at it

vertical frame parallel to angle of the man's left leg (<u>one</u>)

for example, between dimension of black and white squares

name which doesn't matter, an appearance of leaves in motion

and/or landing in a canopy of green branches above (<u>that</u>)

(<u>nothing</u>) except a sound of distance itself, which continues

visibility as the idea of darker ridge below a paler blue

fragment of thought in a white chair (<u>mechanical</u>) going back

to her action, like feeling him not being exactly present

10.21

perception of sky's purple which hasn't appeared (<u>important</u>)

before this, a figure walking toward the closed back door

subject depending on the position of two glasses on the left

whose sound hasn't been included, which (<u>must</u>) also exist

where action takes place, image of color in a plane changing

between observation of it and the point it comes from (<u>p</u>)

(<u>blue</u>) above the intangible surface of a vertical situation,

moment on horizon where light seems to curve toward green

person in last frame not present, (<u>arrangement</u>) of a feeling

according to how it fills the air of otherwise empty room

10.22

interaction of a bird's sound and its shape passing visually

through glass, experienced in terms of this (<u>conjunction</u>)

(blue) green at edge of an about-to-break wave for instance,

whose linear motion the person feels looking back down it

face turned toward viewer, angle as her back leans (<u>paradox</u>)

exactly into the space between his back and opposite wall

duration of notes extended as feeling (situation) continues,

the faded edge of a petal where memory of yellow once was

still below grey-white (surface) texture of sky's dimensions

bounded by apparent weather, man at the table thinking it

10.23

appearance of (concept) across space of room, woman in chair

feeling a picture of two people from somewhere outside it

small bird lifting up from the ground when the second person

(<u>proof</u>) walks toward it, whose meaning isn't itself there

interrupted by a perception of the object and its (position)

behind her, where blue-white above green doesn't continue

sound of feeling it between two shapes, the man's right hand

filling the space in which her features will appear (how)

(<u>something</u>) seems to repeat, like her experience of thinking

reflected in glass beyond the absence of equivalent color

10.24

yellow as motion leaves (picture) it, above which grey-white

and/or blue surface closer to the person who perceives it

absence of wind's sound in passage following (<u>investigation</u>)

elsewhere, notes repeated in back of its insistent return

how the man's shadow appears to be walking toward it, action

looking back through distance after thinking of it (here)

(position) of the woman standing beside table reading letter

in relation to map on wall, whether to turn left or right

act performed by (subject) upon him, how leaves for instance

falling against the blue of apparent sky sound like water

10.25

opacity of leaves through which sun's light passes (subject)

to an image of actual motion, also taking place obliquely

pale blue at lower edge of square (exact) in relation to how

it sounds, where wind moving through air makes it clearer

slant of window's shadow on white wall opposite the observer

whose view of preceding events changes, thus (mechanical)

(action) before an opening scene, where the man falls asleep

followed by entrance of a second person holding something

repetition of bird's sound from the tree's invisible branch,

another descending from its position (picture) near there

10.26

motion of small grey-white body lifting above sand (concept)

for instance, white underside of the soaring bird's wings

window half-open on the left, the vertical edge which frames

a section of ridge below pale blue-white plane of sky (p)

(how) sunlight arrives in the faint reddish glow against it,

relation of distant color into which its shape disappears

visual placement of perpendicular lines in a grid (position)

followed by the sound of notes from another room, example

water falling at farthest corner of house, the (other) woman

to the left of the open window apparently not watching it

10.27

series of three descending notes experienced as (sound) bird

calling from a motion of leaves in wind, overcast feeling

bowl of dried petals next to negative of objects on a table,

(<u>form</u>) in which the distance from first to second changes

diagonal line in left corner (condition) parallel to thought

observed by the person who sees it, beside the white door

hand approaching the plane facing him, head turning to where

she seems to be holding something on left shoulder (<u>this</u>)

(<u>not</u>) action but acoustic shape arriving through translucent

window, orange of nasturtium and/or passion flower's pink

10.28

transparency of drop as water falls from leaf's green (<u>thus</u>)

which isn't its sound, arrival through the eye and/or ear

primrose between the surfaces of a building the color of its

(<u>concept</u>) observation, window plane between it and viewer

waking in a white room beside himself, man who feels absence

connected to second person beyond space of his (<u>thinking</u>)

(<u>nothing</u>) in relation to an object of thought which changes,

silence of darker shapes against opaque grey of the ridge

curve of bone on surface of table to the left (picture) next

to its sound, how the off-stage action doesn't take place

10.29

yellow coming into a green plane, which as pigment dissolves

turns to the person behind a glass watching it (contrast)

(this) thought of color as the woman walks across the floor,

how the position seems to change before its sound arrives

light blue at right edge of the grid adjacent to darker blue

(series) square after which nothing, angle of whose plane

place where (it) sounds, dimension of owl's grey-white wings

when it glides from horizontal line toward grove's shadow

star in blackness of sky above and/or (before) the observer,

whose experience of it continues below the pool's surface

10.30

vertical black lines parallel to three others on left (_that_)

across the feeling of the horizon, red square above white

juxtaposed below the surface, where what happens after first

thinking of an alternative in a different place (_meaning_)

(_x_) for example standing in the foreground's two-dimensional

frame, behind which a corner of the map on the empty wall

displacement of reversed image (_point_) on glass, observation

where the viewer watching the woman's face walks past her

relationship of objects on table in the following (_passage_),

whose colors include citron yellow of a book next to blue

10.31

thought of light passing above (<u>position</u>) of pool's surface,

in whose reflection its appearance isn't exactly observed

moving toward the two-dimensional plane at the top of stairs

below which grey of road goes vertically up to it, (<u>this</u>)

(<u>picture</u>) for instance, yellow on top of white after feeling

profile of woman reading at a table when the man walks in

and/or sound as its shape enters the air (<u>one</u>), first person

imagined as if staring into color of second person's eyes

wingspan of a bird descending on surface of glass, therefore

(<u>possible</u>) the darker green swatch above a bright red one

11.1

pair of birds moving in an otherwise empty blue space of air

whose (<u>two</u>) bodies seem to intersect, which isn't assumed

walking across the road to the man's position (<u>say</u>), how one

left cheek touches another followed by the sound it makes

placed at tip of a branch a drop through which light passes,

which as the wind arrives leaves and/or disappears (<u>fact</u>)

(<u>not</u>) the first person but in relation to him, where feeling

moves from inside the body to its two-dimensional surface

perception of plane in receding space of sound for (<u>example</u>)

including what isn't seen, where off-stage action happens

11.2

angles at which planes of color stand in (physical) relation

to one another, grey adjacent to series of vertical lines

orange at the top edge of a green fence, which isn't exactly

(not) thought of the branch behind it leaning to the left

how for instance the man seems to be leaning toward an image

of its sound, after he (thinks) something has taken place

clouds increasing, curve of buildings at both ends continued

across glass surface toward an illusion of next (picture)

(one) other sequence of notes arriving from the field, sound

which enters as something the viewer doesn't actually see

11.3

curve as plane of road turns right, (<u>how</u>) silence disappears

from the person inside listening as if for the first time

motion of tobacco plant leaves including the following scene

(distance), from which a thought approaches through glass

bird whose sound shapes its absence on a branch for example,

which may or may not be registered as an action (<u>certain</u>)

(<u>that</u>) congruent situation, rectangular blue shape in corner

parallel to her feeling of something happening outside it

view from below corner of building also a possible (<u>picture</u>)

when blackness of night sky is less than visible, perhaps

11.4

yellow places between the veins of a green leaf, for example

presence of feeling (<u>form</u>) below the color of its surface

pattern of birds moving north against ground of the grey sky

which isn't the same in two dimensions, different (angle)

(<u>see</u>) how sound of note shapes feeling in air, where the man

standing beside the grey car is placed in relation to her

light in upstairs window which as a person walks out becomes

the moon's circle, body (<u>imagined</u>) below surface of water

action elsewhere (<u>not</u>) itself visible, how a picture happens

to the person thinking something other than what she sees

269

11.5

relation between sound of a bird's wings falling through air

and the appearance of its shape in a window, where (<u>this</u>)

(<u>point</u>) at which a branch moves, whose body above the person

watching it leaves the afterimage of its motion elsewhere

profile of the woman in a chair also facing left (<u>calculate</u>)

parallel to the distance behind her, which isn't measured

vertical edge of window (<u>a</u>) perpendicular to plane of ridge,

the angle of whose irregular surface intersected by light

motion of man's shadow on a white wall, (<u>object</u>) for example

which isn't quite connected to the person who observes it

11.6

two-dimensional grid of colors in relation to its perception

(<u>simultaneous</u>), reversal of thought back to thinking mind

left hand's weight on grey-white plane of table for example,

which isn't itself the feeling but pictures it (physical)

(<u>line</u>) between a person's left shoulder and blue of her back

turned toward him, horizontal edge of the bottom of a map

film of light grey clouds moving across surface of area (<u>a</u>),

distant edge of a field imagined to approach the observer

opposite reaction along the angle of a green leaf after drop

hits it (<u>defined</u>), an appearance of blue when white opens

11.7

space before which an arrangement of ascending notes (<u>isn't</u>)

exactly resolved, blue light the color of sound's feeling

man on the left (<u>one</u>) whose hand curves across her shoulder,

and/or the girl in the black sweater following that scene

appearance of cloud moving across section of ridge (<u>measure</u>)

the thought of which seems to approach it, not subjective

center of vertical plane the shape of a bird disappears from

for instance, how what happens off stage occurs (perhaps)

(<u>this</u>) action, sound of wind moving against side of building

in relation to how a leaf's motion appears from inside it

11.8

space at the edge where horizontal green rectangle (<u>present</u>)

continues, above which accident of a grey field's feeling

outline of body submerged below plane of the water's surface

imagined from above, clouds moving from north (<u>condition</u>)

(<u>picture</u>) stopped, hummingbird on tip of branch for instance

beyond which distance recedes toward the previous thought

girl's red lips (picture) walking into a room, whose absence

changes the structure of another sound passing through it

position of blue above patches of white another bird's shape

disappears into, followed by (<u>thinking</u>) of its perception

11.9

duration of light (thought) moving from the top of the ridge

toward corner of house behind the viewer, how its silence

following action elsewhere, horizon above which an irregular

(one) shape of a cloud changes from feeling of leaving it

woman in the chair in front of the window beyond which green

appears, where blue of light in the sky isn't (congruent)

(position) of the second person closer than possible thought

moving toward that, and/or sound of body itself breathing

distance between the invisible bird in a field and the sound

it (might) make, followed by motion of shapes on a branch

11.10

color which isn't the feeling inside (action), cells in body

repeated as structure of points on a two-dimensional grid

clouds in left window moving across it (<u>antecedent</u>) that is,

where grey and white become the edge of the present frame

profile of the person whose interior (<u>being</u>) appears as pale

yellow of horizontal plane, the view she sits in front of

absence of the first person, chair to the right of the table

facing the sound of color falling from the sky (physical)

(<u>so</u>) what's happened repeated in thinking about it, the face

turned across the left shoulder toward person watching it

11.11

angle at which tobacco plant leaves the surface of the event

which isn't it, as a feeling of what's inside (knowledge)

(gesture) of her hand reaching back, the woman on whose left

the man who's also present observes in place of an action

time of being in a picture of the grey car before its lights

go out, (how) the sound of a bird arrives after it leaves

person standing at the table reading a letter, which (means)

it's happened rather than where a visual fact takes place

blue square in upper right corner whose position (p) repeats

thinking of it, as seeing which is also said of its shape

11.12

feeling approach of colder air from the outside being action

(itself), smell of smoke in the man on the right's breath

color of ridge changing from (_real_) to imagined observation,

as a person on the telephone watches light in a room fade

position of body below surface of pool, which isn't thinking

in relation to (_what_) happens in the color surrounding it

pale yellow space of building between darker shapes of trees

adjacent to the woman facing opposite direction, (figure)

(object) passing across the man's field of view for instance

pair of hummingbirds, which in following scenes disappear

11.13

smell of woman's neck (<u>here</u>), the position of the man's hand

continuous as a memory of the feeling where it touched it

back turned to the window out which sound of traffic happens

(fact) opposite direction of a branch, which leaves color

first person leaving the car looks back, sees its headlights

as the presence of a thought that follows it (phenomenon)

(<u>under</u>) influence of it, the man's situation being performed

as a physical action whose parts include reaching forward

distance between an interior space (<u>one</u>) and what's outside,

the figure walking behind him who isn't therefore present

11.14

direction as line crosses a feeling of (<u>one</u>) two-dimensional

space of field, blurred figure of man above white surface

rectangular floor, painting reflecting its image on the wall

between pair of windows whose traffic sounds (assumption)

(<u>being</u>) woman striking first left then right cheek, opposite

diagonal running from lower left edge to thought of green

grey of blue tones whose sound is an effect of what happened

previously, (<u>sense</u>) of dream approaching through its mind

table at the far end of the room, therefore an interior view

(<u>unprovable</u>) in which the subject will end up in the book

11.15

man walking down set of stairs viewed from his left (_itself_)

entrance, which includes the saturation of blue and green

light at corner of window (_how_) through which edge of bridge

beyond a series of cars whose sound arrives, for instance

vertical landscape turned on its side, white where something

scraped horizontal lines on expanse of red feeling (_this_)

(_position_) of man on left in relation to largeness of figure

leaning toward him, which continues in the negative space

hand on window's frame perpendicular to line on wall (blank)

preceded by black above a grey field, after which nothing

11.16

vertical (<u>angle</u>) lines of bamboo behind orange of nasturtium

which appears to hang in air, whose surface isn't feeling

motion from one set of spellings to another whose (meanings)

aren't the same, because its sound will also have changed

subject as her hand goes out to stop the man on the sidewalk

stepping into oncoming blue car, (<u>calculation</u>) as content

color disappearing from landscape, grey in relation to black

on the walls of a white room whose surface leaves (<u>there</u>)

(picture) actual face whose interior presence isn't measured

looking over the folds of her left shoulder, behind which

11.17

perception of horizontal curve (<u>abstracted</u>) which disappears

when blue comes into it, in relation to that event itself

and/or how first person sees it, sound of the ocean (series)

outside the example of waves advancing on invisible shore

nothing that isn't said of orange arriving at a cloud's edge

following edge whose color wraps around yellow, (<u>concept</u>)

(dimension) of light, action in a drop that falls from green

pine branch next to bird the viewer sees landing above it

right hand positioned on table below vertical black (<u>system</u>)

line, beyond which yellow and blue projection of interior

11.18

distance between passion vine's red and the leaves behind it

(<u>system</u>) of sound, nasturtium's orange reflected in glass

surface of action whose meaning is itself an acoustic event,

the sound of the car's image passing in the street (<u>here</u>)

(<u>this</u>) initiative ceded to words, a shadow of leaves falling

against the rectangular blue square in upper right corner

feeling in the woman's mouth (<u>not</u>) leaving, which isn't what

she thinks of looking at the relation of colors in a grid

pale blue above darkness of green in window opposite an idea

for instance, absence of light (<u>concept</u>) at side of cheek

11.19

sunlight on a branch in which the shape of a bird (position)

stops followed by another and another, who also disappear

sequence of three notes descending, where sound means (<u>what</u>)

things are happening outside thought of green and/or blue

woman walking into the room after something has taken place,

which includes her feeling in relation to walls (picture)

(<u>picture</u>) of color framed in a window, width of word's event

whose sound arrives as a dimension placed in viewer's eye

horizontal blackness across (<u>a</u>) lower edge of vertical plane

behind which thought itself, pale yellow petals in a bowl

11.20

motion where patches of bamboo leaves in front of the viewer

(<u>one</u>) shift as a yellow-throated bird lands, for instance

line continued to the right side of the page, from which (<u>x</u>)

sound rises as the second person walks back into the room

triangular green shape of absence behind the boy facing away

from her (<u>question</u>), intersected by curve of idea's frame

object in the observer's eye in relation to space around it,

whereas the feeling of action seems to happen inside (<u>it</u>)

(<u>spatial</u>) texture of the horizontal green area perpendicular

to green below it, each of which contains a sense of blue

11.21

shadow across side of a hill (glance) from building on left,

the vertical presence of whose colors continues beyond it

shape of leaves on branch in glass, through which it arrives

coincident with descending notes in adjacent room (after)

(a) the person across the table turning left, who rearranges

the position of the man's words from one place to another

feeling of grey plane above tobacco plant's green (variable)

surfaces understood as a thought happens, exactly present

disappearance of bird (b) at edge of picture, where thinking

becomes a grey-white film in front of the invisible ridge

11.22

pink-orange of petals on a table after (<u>logic</u>) color itself,

below which horizontal band of darker orange beside black

man's actions on beach in relation to what's going on inside

the observer's head (<u>example</u>), woman in front of a mirror

back of shoulders turned toward the figure reading it, glass

lagoon's surface scored by thought of bird landing (<u>like</u>)

(<u>this</u>) reflection, one red square changing into the next one

followed by the feeling of being beside the person waking

blue area above the white corner of cloud which isn't itself

moving, (<u>how</u>) events might sound by means of such letters

11.23

red square next to the larger black (<u>one</u>), ratio of material

letters on the page to the person's motion in her clothes

light on white wall reflected in glass behind viewer (<u>being</u>)

the appearance of a speaking subject, which doesn't exist

horizontal windows closed, sounds coming in from the outside

surface of building (<u>grammatical</u>) a perception of weather

placement of dark green square between the pages of the book

for instance, whose position isn't a conscious (<u>decision</u>)

(<u>how</u>) flag in wind is action, the girl walking into the room

in relation to the man who looks up at what's she's doing

11.24

space at the edge of a roof where the drop falls (structure)

followed by another, whose feeling it continues to embody

white cloud moving across a pale blue field of sky in window

in relation to profile of the figure facing it, (concept)

(not) actually present, when she returns to the door the man

thinks to open into memory of being somewhere before that

motion in clump the bird leaves (empirical), next to thought

whose color is itself filled with the sound of blue-green

face looking back over shoulder, detail of (first) man's arm

reaching toward the figure whose back is therefore turned

11.25

sound coming in from outside (picture) bird missing, surface

of tobacco plant leaves in the grey of air surrounding it

woman not present in room making the shape of the man's body

change (physical), condition of which observed from above

petals on table turning from pink-orange to yellow-brown (x)

without the experience of a feeling, previous interaction

series of rectangular forms juxtaposed in the vertical plane

perceived as an arrangement of color itself, (imaginable)

(logic) for instance, window through which an action arrives

when the person stops looking at the texture of the ridge

11.26

absence of color in cloud (<u>defined</u>) before sun hits, whereas

the inside of the flower in the window begins to turn red

triangular rock positioned on top of the large one (another)

off-stage action, man picking grass from cracks in bricks

notes in the next room continued, including shape of thought

which sounds like swells rising to twenty-two feet (here)

(<u>possibility</u>) of second person standing at the table in blue

against the map on the wall, edge which intersects letter

memory of bird gliding from left to right (<u>calculus</u>) without

moving its wings, which isn't the actual perception of it

11.27

dark green shape of tree moving against grey of adjacent sky

as wind arrives, (<u>different</u>) yellow leaves falling in air

blank of wall opposite the viewer (<u>a</u>), whose feeling changes

in relation to the distance between him and second person

right hand placed on edge of table below vertical black line

which intersects pale yellow or blue beyond it, (<u>measure</u>)

(angle) a bird's sound approaches from outside left, pattern

of the woman's action not shifting in the following scene

interior dimension of thought itself, example (<u>mathematical</u>)

perceived as concentric spheres of its sound and/or color

11.28

faded green paint on the wall of an adjacent house (forward)

sound of an invisible bird continued, somewhere behind it

second person standing against the trunk of an enormous tree

(<u>construction</u>), followed by woman who stops to imagine it

horizontal green plane (<u>result</u>), example of pale blue square

whose feeling becomes an exterior surface seen from above

film of the man who enters the room through a smashed window

in relation to color, that such an act happens (position)

(<u>one</u>) profile of the woman facing left, left arm pulled back

toward shadow in whose thinking the viewer doesn't appear

11.29

circle on plane of pool's surface when the first drop falls,

contour of the invisible body below moving toward it (<u>in</u>)

(<u>then</u>) outside dimension of largest tree compared to the man

who's inside it, thinking of what takes place before that

grey-white cloud between shadow of ridge and viewer, (<u>exact</u>)

outline of small birds gliding into physical shape of air

person beside the woman below (<u>possible</u>) sound at the window

which wakes him, an action of wind and/or rain's approach

rectangular pale blue feeling in lower left corner (<u>mistake</u>)

passing the house behind the fence, absence of connection

11.30

reflection of light on forehead (_experience_) opposite window

through whose surface the sound of air, as motion arrives

figure in chair on right holding the white cup to her mouth,

which isn't the feeling of the blue-white wall (_language_)

(_calculation_) for example, appearance of first diagonal line

perceived in relation to where its shape intersects color

warmth pulling across the man's shoulder in the dark (_white_)

transition, before which violent action of tobacco leaves

profile of (_other_) woman in glass, thought itself continuous

where the subject who thinks it happens and/or disappears

12.1

surprise of child with large shoulders walking into the room

(blue), as to whether he is actually present or elsewhere

cars parked perpendicular (confusion) to curve of green road

below which rounded shape of tree, which isn't exactly it

prone position of ridge at far edge of field (psychological)

before light, how the bird's sound just appears to happen

person standing beside the door, where an experience follows

an emotion toward or away from its sense of being (clear)

(order) of objects in a related scene including how she sits

facing left, window of adjacent building reflecting light

12.2

interval between the bird's sound and what the observer sees

landing on a bare stalk above corner of fence, (<u>describe</u>)

(<u>it</u>) like that, in that what happens after it stops thinking

becomes an action in the grey-white fog which blankets it

horizontal blue of sky above the profile of the woman's head

feeling disappears, (<u>not</u>) knowing or being one and/or two

leaves, a thought before the word parenthesis whose (<u>effect</u>)

becomes the dark green color below his recollection of it

absence of trees in a cloud's shape (<u>symptom</u>) not perceived,

daylight being the time when a visible action takes place

297

12.3

ratio of faint blue patch in upper left corner of the window

(present) to position of cloud around it, which continues

robin's size, alone (without) the person having witnessed it

therefore moving from thought to branch of an absent tree

gate which opens included in its sound, image of girl's face

where it turns and/or looks back over blue shoulder (see)

(experience) subject by itself, edge of sunlight followed by

various green surfaces of leaves through which it arrives

interior view of action which happens elsewhere (mechanical)

to the second person, something which isn't in fact there

12.4

sound before appearance of leaves moving on an actual branch

outside window, how (that) happens in chronological space

vertical plane of pale yellow building propped against glass

in relation to which a person sees himself, watching (it)

(how) scale of an object changes, color approaching a viewer

in whose perception of greenish yellow its feeling occurs

hummingbird as it leaves a lavender's purple flower, (under)

which point of entrance into corresponding edge of bricks

thought which follows it (in) fact, as if a rhythm of events

takes place in the time between one sensation and another

12.5

appearance of a thread-like strand (one) when sunlight hits,

stretched between diagonal of branch and a vertical stalk

acoustic shapes in air, possible angle of translucent planes

(not) exactly observable from the man's position above it

events in the foreground which correspond to thoughts moving

contrapuntally, (what) happens between two or more voices

sound at curved edge of nasturtium's green for instance, how

grey-white enters the performance where blue was (before)

(function), detail in which a figure looks over her shoulder

and/or reaches the right hand across left corner of a map

12.6

pattern of small birds moving from one color to next glimpse

through blue frame of window, walking past its (position)

(<u>indirect</u>) object of thinking which happens in light itself,

angle of sun as it rises behind bamboo and/or pine branch

landscape outside the window, including a motion of the wind

(<u>not</u>) making its way into sound of contralto in next room

yellow square on right adjacent to (<u>simple</u>) blue rectangular

feeling possible, man facing viewer against plane of rock

reaching back, left arm lifted toward nearly horizontal line

interrupted by the idea of seeing (<u>it</u>) inside the picture

12.7

visual action of person moving above (<u>content</u>) second person

for example, where moonlight seems to come down from left

underside of bird's white wings, whose disappearance follows

(<u>actual</u>) perception of emerging green on surface of ridge

feeling in wall behind diagonal edge of darker shape on left

intersected by observer's experience of it, (<u>proposition</u>)

(<u>being</u>) where grey light begins, opposite identity of planes

against which an image of thought itself seems to project

blue in upper right corner in relation to (<u>how</u>) hand touches

texture of other side, which isn't exactly apparent to it

12.8

linear series of sounds whose action happens (<u>spontaneously</u>)

as follows, overhead view of wings against grid of bricks

distance between window's plane and thinking of its exterior

surface as line in relation to shape and color, (<u>concept</u>)

(<u>so</u>) image that takes place, left hand holding edge of paper

upon which words suggest something has previously occured

silence after the last note's possibility, faint white (<u>one</u>)

grey cloud behind reflection of interior in glass on left

body of person in foreground lying face down in blood, exact

point of view (<u>part</u>) depending on position of an observer

12.9

see rotation of diagonal line from upper left to lower right

edge (optical), the head facing in the opposite direction

figure bending over as if to touch something not seen, (say)

horizontal green surface leaning against colors in a grid

angle of whose hand (is) it, the idea of a physical presence

appearing in relation to the visibility of negative space

known as an arrangement of events which surround its absence

in the first place, which is in itself a form of (seeing)

(position) of hand across table for example, after she turns

around to look back over her shoulder directly toward him

12.10

whitish-pink of clouds reflected on glass surface (a) viewed

through angle of a perpendicular window, where it changes

possiblility, as if the color coming into it happens between

the action and the time in which it arrives (calculation)

(of) feeling in the motionless bird above the field, subject

unspoken moving from the lower left to upper right corner

something like blue scrawled across portion of sky (picture)

example, memory of the figure watching man in water below

hesitation within the vulnerable body a (form) of its visual

and/or acoustic dimension, motion of leaves without sound

12.11

and/or not moving, horizontal arrangement of negative images

positioned on a table beyond which green isn't (<u>reversed</u>)

(<u>one</u>) close-up of bird landing on sill followed by its sound

leaving, the body lighting up the space it seemed to fill

memory of action from exterior point of view (<u>not</u>) therefore

exactly fixed, projection of deer's shape into the future

example of car passing in the street outside the fence (<u>one</u>)

after which it stops, opposite the example of its silence

string hanging into space instead of painting (<u>that</u>) becomes

awareness of feeling circularity, being itself like color

12.12

body whose absence includes the feeling of space (<u>calculate</u>)

into which it disappears, as sky turns from pink to white

interior of memory looking (<u>over</u>) shoulder, immediate action

between man in the chair and his sense of person speaking

triangular blue plane in relation to curve of passion vine's

green surface, shape of parenthesis inside of which (<u>one</u>)

(<u>less</u>) than visible events, horizontal motion from the right

as the wingspan of a bird glides down over plane of water

simultaneity of the feeling parallel to (<u>its</u>) physical body,

thought of which seems to arrive from the edge of a fence

12.13

water poured against rocks in corner from which steam rises,

memory of second person breathing (_its_) additional motion

grey-white feeling between (_object_) horizontal body of ridge

and the sound of a bird which moves through it, inaudible

crows on branch above the street for instance, woman in blue

(standing) opposite the map whose right corner is missing

action of the girl in the doorway adjacent to man whose hand

holds her shoulder, as an event which isn't present (_one_)

(_pure_) awareness of itself, where the plane of color changes

an acoustic phenomenon into the surface it happens inside

12.14

interval between the sounds (it) makes and shape of the bird

landing on a branch, and/or how that isn't exactly action

moon's crescent visible through tobacco plant leaves (<u>there</u>)

for example, which determines viewer's emotional distance

motion of horizontal lines from left to right corner of grid

whose presence includes what happens elsewhere, (picture)

(<u>picture</u>) of man standing against slab of rock, the unspoken

subject of thought measured in terms of what surrounds it

window as light comes into it, (<u>what</u>) takes place after that

continued into the positive space of the still empty room

12.15

angle of rock's corner above which the blue of sky beyond it

(<u>here</u>) echoes the man's shoulder, left of opposite shadow

blue texture of figure reading letter, profile (<u>p</u>) from left

which implies the presence of a viewer who doesn't appear

previous action of two butterflies (concept) locked together

in place, diagonal lines of wings' shadows against bricks

surface of water in the green glass into which stem plunges,

negative plane whose feeling is leaning against it (<u>away</u>)

(<u>this</u>) disappearance of sound for instance, an opposite note

which approaches person waking in upstairs room elsewhere

12.16

yellow curve of road bending vertically to the right, series

of cars parked perpendicular to thought of its (position)

(<u>inside</u>) gate, beyond which action of stairs going up toward

the man stopped at the door through which he doesn't walk

blue square in the middle of green adjacent to another (<u>one</u>)

after the telephone rings, an articulation of her feeling

relation of the body to the color it lies in (fact) observed

by person who enters from right, side of the face covered

emotion filling an interior of sound, leaves a space outside

(<u>significance</u>) in which a second person can also be heard

12.17

feeling in the color for instance blood, image reversed (<u>is</u>)

as if sound approaches the fence between house and street

edge of sun through green distance (<u>where</u>) blue passes above

shape of tree, memory of a bird landing and/or leaving it

woman behind grid of tones whose right arm extends to corner

(picture) on the wall of invisible action perhaps, or not

object seen, its thought therefore continued into the middle

distance in which the body at the table isn't (<u>different</u>)

(<u>that</u>) starting with what's written, hear where a sound goes

after the telephone rings and the person leaves a message

12.18

bird (<u>unknown</u>) passing from right in front of the horizontal

dimension of ridge, beyond whose depth the blue-white air

edge of something before feeling arrives, where apprehension

coincides with the shape of emotion happening inside (<u>it</u>)

(<u>image</u>) instead of its sound, crow on cypress branch calling

back and forth across space between one idea and the next

figure in a chair whose back is facing the window (<u>language</u>)

in which green parallels the grey of distance, not seeing

changing light and shadow on bamboo leaves as the wind moves

through it, first person (<u>p</u>) hearing the negative of 'no'

12.19

perception of bird itself moving through the bamboo thicket,

action happening (between) an event and its disappearance

feeling's duration ($\underline{x}$) after which the second person refuses

to participate, in which sound enters a spatial dimension

outside the window on the left, distance from the horizontal

green plane of ridge below which shapes are passing (one)

(part) thinking in relation to the physical body which takes

place inside figure seated at table, light on yellow rose

experience as the subject arrives from elsewhere, man (form)

standing in front of rock whose crack slants to the right

12.20

simultaneity of the grey-white body (<u>not</u>) moving above field

and the vertical surface beyond it, where snow has fallen

crows calling across space between cypress branch and viewer

who doesn't see the second of two shapes ascending, (<u>one</u>)

(<u>it</u>) followed by presence of letters in otherwise empty air,

which changes the listener's experience into memory of it

position relative to the second person, not (<u>in</u>) front of it

but an opposite action of landscape leaning against glass

conclusion of thought itself moving from left across (logic)

inside a sequence of events, which doesn't in fact happen

12.21

turning back over her left shoulder, (<u>how</u>) the tobacco plant

leaves sound in space between departure and disappearance

blue of curve stretching toward distance (<u>it</u>) makes present,

when the person in the foreground isn't actually thinking

observation of two figures in adjacent building for instance

perpendicular to the moment it occurs, which isn't (<u>only</u>)

(<u>what</u>) happens inside it, assuming the subject whose feeling

originates in the shadow behind the ridge might be spoken

light filtered through translucent green, relation (<u>that</u>) is

to acoustic shape of words which enter the listener's ear

12.22

motion in dark outside glass, edges of a branch which change

position relative to the source of light behind him (how)

(that) person walking across a field of wind-flattened grass

seen from a distance, sound of color like ridge beyond it

green square on left edge below blue of rectangle (example),

an experience of whose vertical presence includes feeling

space between arrival of grey light through a random pattern

(defined) of leaves and perception of it, figure at table

paler blue above the ridge which isn't (this) thought, tawny

color of plane behind profile of the woman parallel to it

12.23

pairs of smaller shapes darting between glass (and) vertical

shadow of still dark fence, which isn't about description

how (it) appears in black and/or white, either inside memory

or the surface of an object whose volume occupies thought

air moving through leaves which themselves change (position)

for example, not an experience of emotion but being in it

three birds perched on a bare stalk between green of passion

vines and paler blue of the sky above it, not named (not)

(more) than sound itself, observation of acoustic phenomenon

including crow on the cypress branch calling the listener

12.24

film of grey-white clouds above bird on tobacco plant branch

(<u>thus</u>), which leaves the moment perception shifts to next

action of wave breaking seen from inside it, how the falling

blue-green surface meets the horizontal plane (<u>following</u>)

(<u>at</u>) oblique angle to it, top of tree in relation to outside

corner of room in which it becomes second source of light

sound filtered through (<u>this</u>) motion of wind in bamboo, thus

thicket where the silence happens between image and glass

blue shape of figure whose back faces viewer's line of sight

for example (<u>form</u>), when thought approaches from the left

12.25

profile of girl from below angle of ridge (<u>also</u>) not talking

able to see above the emotion, instead of being inside it

horizontal plane of field (form) for instance, second person

moving forward ahead of figure whose thought includes her

ambient sound at porch of man's ear, in relation to distance

between appearance of wave breaking and its (description)

(<u>is</u>) itself seen, where leaves take place in black and white

shadow of image on wall at left of blue and/or yellow bed

first person submerged in pool (<u>one</u>) below half-open window,

beside which the color of sand echoes the frame around it

12.26

image arriving from outside left, simultaneity of blue-green

dimension of water from above and/or surface level (fact)

(<u>is</u>) action happening below where edge of ground drops away,

visual perception of bird after the first person hears it

position of small white subject on bare branch which (<u>isn't</u>)

exactly it, feeling itself in relation to space around it

grey scale (<u>that</u>) is appearance of object above top of ridge

followed by example of figure's interior motion, thinking

horizontal green area below blue square, whose diagonal line

(<u>is</u>) descending from the upper left to lower right corner

12.27

particle too small to be seen by itself, action (experience)

in which the man's leg sinks below surface of pool's dark

smoke coming into the room whose shape (is) black and white,

before the viewer's perception of color becomes saturated

blackish-green angle of trees below flat space where emotion

isn't exactly pronounced, sound of (one) and/or two crows

two figures on left through glass, picture whose alternative

is a physical sensation in which orange and yellow (play)

(what) follows, how the second person approaching the window

disappears into a series of more or less descending notes

12.28

clouds in moonlight which (<u>could</u>) be arriving through window

whose afterimage is silver, around which a multiple frame

interval between emotion and the person on the left feeling,

who continues turning himself over inside it (<u>imaginable</u>)

(<u>a</u>) color in relation to action, the second person listening

when the bird's sound comes into the room's white silence

allusion to parallel lines on floor (<u>count</u>), telephone wires

in the two-dimensional plane of painting against the wall

source of light behind a reflection of the second person (<u>p</u>)

opposite window, stars beyond physical sensation of ridge

12.29

and/or out the door above it (_knowledge_), sound of the woman

standing to the right of the table above which map's edge

yellow rectangle in lower corner of grid through which light

doesn't actually pass, diagonal line of sight (_interpret_)

(_so_) how the child in the white dress looks between parents,

looking for example at an object in the middle of her lap

orange globes in the foreground, whose sense isn't (_related_)

to the feeling of an emotion happening inside man on left

first of two black windows (_posed_) behind her head, possible

color of the wall above it framing woman who doesn't talk

324

12.30

counter-rotation of the picture's vertical plane (position),

followed by appearance of woman on black and white screen

bird's shape passing below grey cloud in the middle distance

(figure) for instance, another landing on a bamboo branch

feeling of parallel lines, paler blue in white above horizon

whose sound includes the following series of words (then)

(under) action of younger person leaning to her right behind

other's shoulder, thought of whom continues in next frame

perception of air around subject (here), whose visible green

motion happens in the time it takes an observer to see it

12.31

middle of three rectangular windows implied, gesture of hand

reaching across edge of perpendicular corner (phenomenon)

(action) inside it, the person on the left sitting up in bed

for whom an object is shaped by the silence it arrives in

horizontal green (position) below which landscape of thought

disappears, dimension of grey sky above an adjacent house

absence of body whose feeling includes its sound (<u>possible</u>),

second color in relation to the field which doesn't exist

first person next to window followed by description, surface

(<u>thing</u>) continued into the paler blue space of background

1.1

subject of sentence (fact) positioned after previous action,

figure on left having expressed an opposite point of view

reflected in glass through which angle of corner image (<u>one</u>)

in which yellows and/or greens intersect, adjacent events

blue-white surface of water (example) whose thought includes

experience next to it, interior to sound of second person

white of motion above it, horizontal line between lower blue

plane and shape of color falling toward it (<u>circumstance</u>)

(<u>that</u>) relation between figures in front of window, vertical

dimension of the frame after which something else happens

1.2

structure of the scene whose action includes this afterimage

(being) of sound, preceding the experience of an observer

distance between color of rock and the blue-white (position)

surface of wave breaking against it, invisible body below

length of parallel lines to the left, apparently interrupted

by related series of sounds following one after (another)

(condition) of event in which second person thinks something

happens before it, blue on the right recognized as yellow

feeling in that person (grammar) changed into an observation

exterior to motion of clouds from the north, for instance

1.3

degree to which the mental picture changes color of (<u>plane</u>),

possible effect of action continued after its sound stops

paler blue-white above glass, vertical position of left hand

where thinking happens between absence of ridge and (<u>not</u>)

(body) of horizontal plane intersected by the angle of light

slanting across it, second syllable on the following page

relation between the closer of two figures in the background

(<u>mechanical</u>) and a motion of sand, man in middle distance

perception of an action determined by (<u>how</u>) one remembers it

after it disappears, an interruption of line on the floor

329

1.4

grey-white of a bird after it leaves the left window, person

on whose left a reflection of two triangular shapes (<u>one</u>)

(<u>a</u>) vertical line above the **upper right** corner of the table,

where the woman might place **the feeling** in her right hand

following perception of subject (thought), older man walking

through space of actual room beyond which flat blue plane

horizontal green before the exterior dimension of two colors

(comparison) one of which is white, prior to first person

after sound arrives, relation of object to its departure (<u>p</u>)

approximate to second color floating in a pale background

1.5

sound coming forward to become (<u>analysis</u>) an adjacent object

for instance, how the name of a bird next door disappears

left profile of figure next to the table in front of the man

facing the viewer on a bench (here), child in white dress

feeling of color through branches of trees, whose appearance

changes the landscape (<u>1</u>) in relation to action inside it

green tendrils wrapping around a strand of barbed wire, word

positioned above the line whose sound it is thinking (<u>of</u>)

(<u>like</u>) woman on child's left, angle of the arm perpendicular

to the horizontal motion of thought beside the ochre wall

1.6

motion at the curled edges of a leaf, where the sun comes up

(fact) of first person waking beside memory of the second

sound of object experienced as a feeling of space around it,

the perceiver's body turning toward it in the dark (<u>here</u>)

(<u>how</u>) it happens, image of the action followed by the letter

behind the woman's back toward which the man then reaches

performance of the previous action on the person approaching

from right foreground, who is then (being) closer to whom

bird against blue-white sky after its sound arrives, subject

who wants him to take it (<u>geometrical</u>) not holding it out

1.7

monotone at porch of ear, yellow ochre in upper right corner

(<u>situation</u>) adjacent to where silence enters from outside

sunlight on the vertical plane opposite (<u>consequence</u>) moment

two figures walking toward it, one approximate to another

actual position of the man on her left for example, apparent

motion of pool's surface caused by bodies below it (view)

(<u>this</u>) following the subject upon which action is performed,

grey-white feeling above the horizontal line of the ridge

thinking of color as (<u>logic</u>) moves through it, where absence

changes his idea of himself into the arrival of its sound

1.8

difference between the object of thought and thinking of it,

fog's silence moving across patches of passion vine (and)

(and) before it, subject of the blue-white field above whose

horizontal dimension the feeling of absence comes to rest

appearance of emotion against the adjacent plane which stops

(this) placement of one thing beside another, for example

before the person hears it, ear's perception of sound (said)

of the acoustic shape of two crows calling back and forth

lighter surface of tobacco plant leaves in relation to green

of bamboo thicket behind it, which (acts) connected to it

1.9

color coming into sky above the horizontal line of the ridge

(r) which isn't it, followed by a memory of related sound

intersection of person's approach to the table (phenomenon),

an exterior condition of the intangible object being read

feeling inside (not) observed, where two-dimensional pattern

of shadow falls against the front wall of different house

how blue and/or green of landscape leans across glass, first

person speaking of an action which happens before it (or)

(act) of previous sensation itself, woman in back of the man

who doesn't see the lights below where the grey car turns

1.10

lower curve of moon tipped over from (<u>one</u>) view to the next,

the person not knowing why a previous action has happened

followed by its emotion, second interior event whose subject

continues the presence and/or reappearance of color (<u>two</u>)

(different) possible interval between the approach of second

or first letter, pale blue-white through which owl sounds

horizontal line of thought (<u>effect</u>) against which man's head

faces the person in front of it, whose perception changes

position of observer in relation to memory of feeling inside

(<u>where</u>) subject of thinking itself arrives, example of it

1.11

vertical yellow shape on left perpendicular to how its sound

(would) appear, back of woman's head turned toward window

plane moving across depth of blue distance followed by (act)

building on the side of the ridge, an acoustic perception

angle of rock's surface, direction of grey and/or white bird

previous to where one perched in the top of the tree (is)

(concept) in itself, physical condition of thin white clouds

in relation to second person's memory of interior feeling

slope above the observer (also) white, thought of horizontal

placement of left hand in front of the dark blue shoulder

1.12

green of tobacco plant branch in motion where the bird lands

followed by another, left side of the painting (<u>physical</u>)

(<u>is</u>) placed next to it, light appearing through darker green

adjacent pine the feeling of which isn't exactly observed

leaning to the left above horizontal plane for example, (<u>it</u>)

parallel to birds landed on telephone wire prior to sound

and/or before it, appearance of (<u>one</u>) person's hand on table

below a vertical black line which seems to divide thought

head of the second figure leaning toward man's left shoulder

in a previous scene, (<u>his</u>) memory of which follows action

1.13

reflection in window of the perpendicular wall (possibility)

when observer looks up, thought facing opposite direction

absence of its physical shape (one) once bird leaves, viewer

whose interior feeling changes the dimension of the object

air in relation to the motion of leaves in a vertical window

(that) is itself continuous, pale blue and white above it

orange below the surface of the adjacent rectangular object,

the angle from which certain action itself follows (this)

(how) its sound occurs, interaction of colors in left corner

previous to what the listener at the table actually hears

1.14

girl looking over right shoulder (<u>not</u>) present, white of fog

at the edge of a field parallel to line of ridge above it

feeling inside the following notes, as action moves in space

between an upper and lower dimension of color (calculate)

(possible) condition of a building beyond which nothing else

appears, how hearing becomes the object of related sounds

vertical arrangement of colors in plane including pale blue,

black and/or (<u>white</u>) image of hand around the man's waist

prior to reverse motion, example of subject in car (<u>observe</u>)

approaching location of events previous to thinking of it

1.15

thought in which motion of the horizontal plane stops (<u>one</u>),

after which the action of the subject on the left happens

figure talking on right (triangle) not the same as the event

for instance, grey and/or blue of floor tilting toward it

reflection of color in water's surface, body moving under it

itself beside or in front of the person who observes (it)

(example) detail of the table at the edge of which the woman

sits in front of pale yellow, glass on square below light

relation of sound approaching through the window on the left

(position) to something the person doesn't hear, possible

1.16

body of thought, pale blue of plane across which bird exists

before the sound it makes approaching the listener (here)

(picture) in front of the person reading in black and white,

nothing surrounding the observer but shape of its feeling

thinking of breathing in adjacent room, following horizontal

(position) of arm across waist of figure at edge of table

darker green surface of the ridge which (is) actually before

the color of an action above it arrives, without thinking

glass in middle distance between the subject and (something)

taking place inside it, car driving in opposite direction

1.17

juxtaposition of sound ($\underline{x}$) beside the listener who thinks it

happens somewhere else, whereas its motion occurs outside

woman walking across room at oblique angle ($\underline{a}$) to the person

turning toward other man, to whom feeling isn't connected

surface of opposite wall in relation to horizontal plane ($\underline{p}$)

in front of it, grey-white fog above the approaching tree

parallel blue lines facing the viewer, prior adjacent action

of the white wall moving to the left of the window (here)

(subject) shapes gathered where the sound of an event enters

dimension of a flat black room, location of which follows

1.18

syncopated motion of a branch as water falls from roof above

it (logic), beyond which corner of the perpendicular wall

yellow below a distant vertical plane, figure in front of it

into whose interior world the object is projected (<u>sense</u>)

(evidence) of outside event determined by the sound it makes

in flat grey light, knowing the shape of what isn't there

man in black and white reflected on the wall behind (<u>action</u>)

viewer facing in opposite direction, arm resting on floor

form of being in it (<u>picture</u>), triangular green wedge before

and/or in back of the person on the left who thinks of it

1.19

looking over left shoulder (<u>movement</u>) after which an emotion

followed by the approach of off-stage action, for example

birds lined up on telephone wire, (<u>how</u>) it becomes the sound

projected onto the listener who hears it passing overhead

blue square in relation to adjacent green above it, in which

an interior feeling of physical motion happens (position)

(<u>is</u>) it, the landscape in the window echoed by an appearance

related to the color of a branch and/or the sky beyond it

person looking through plane at (<u>is</u>) preceding action, where

thinking continues subject to the next or following event

1.20

detail of a bird's sound repeated on left, object positioned

in the upper right corner in relation to its image (<u>that</u>)

(<u>form</u>) of action corresponding to the man's perception of it

in the following scene, body standing beside an empty bed

light on green surfaces of leaves (<u>in</u>) slow motion, followed

by grey above the horizontal plane of the invisible field

thought of woman standing next to table in lower left corner

whose feeling (<u>is</u>) implied, blue-white waist against wall

yellow below the line between it and orange shape above (<u>it</u>)

for example, separation of the first and/or second person

1.21

temporal dimension between the plane of the ridge and (<u>this</u>)

parallel white lines, color beyond which action continues

walking into room beside (<u>same</u>) person, the man for instance

reacting to the sound to her voice reading words about it

light changing appearance of branch surrounded by its motion

in space, condition of figure (<u>in</u>) the chair on the right

behind which green below yellow, following thought of events

repeated in the feeling of the object next to it or (<u>not</u>)

(<u>his</u>) experience in relation to vertical edge between walls,

perspective in moving toward and/or away from the subject

1.22

thought before the physical object for example, calculus ($\underline{x}$)

of color outside window followed by an image of its sound

position of first person in front of wall behind whom action

continues, vertical black lines between which yellow ($\underline{is}$)

($\underline{this}$) feeling before the subject, rotation of perpendicular

green and/or blue spaces of area repeated in what follows

event in which the person turned away from the window thinks

something fills the invisible plane beyond ($\underline{it}$), not seen

darker edge of leaves ($\underline{in}$) grey light, negative of its space

from which an angle changes in relation to wall beyond it

1.23

figure in field repeated as to position of feeling around it

(that) is, perception related to idea of man on the right

disappearance of the body into closed space, after (gesture)

event on the diagonal plane when second person approaches

previous figure's position following the object which occurs

to the right of it, which continues to move away from (x)

(point) above or beside it, line between edge of the picture

and thinking of what takes place before an action happens

color of the adjacent vertical plane (p) in relation to what

doesn't actually appear, detail of sound as physical fact

1.24

shadow whose motion on the pale green wall of adjacent house

isn't acoustic, followed by the sound of water which (<u>is</u>)

(<u>this</u>) thinking, how the subject actually takes place before

and/or after it occurs in the space of the previous scene

arrangement of objects on opposite wall related to (<u>picture</u>)

arrival of its sound, woman on the left walking toward it

leaves in front of what happens, (<u>one</u>) to the left of action

beside it prior to when things are simply being described

interior of person facing the wall, actual position on floor

(<u>not</u>) repetition of event at different place in landscape

1.25

grey-white of cloud above horizontal line of the ridge (two)

whose sound isn't present, shape of bird moving across it

memory not of action but thing itself, the person leaving it

(as) a letter on the ground by the car parked in the dark

blue square in the upper right corner in relation to profile

positioned next to the table (fact), which seems to occur

surrounded by silence of green leaves, right hand below line

which divides yellow from plane adjacent to it (possible)

(shape) thought whose actual feeling appears to exist inside

first person, action of the second bird landing in a bush

1.26

interval between positions of color on the horizontal branch

(physical) in relation to branch behind it, which follows

same green leaves in a different place, how the yellow below

and/or above it will also thus appear to exist (<u>possible</u>)

(<u>image</u>) of person thinking before the object, thought itself

when a bird disappears into a thicket of peripheral color

sound of action beyond the closed white door which continues

(<u>picture</u>), perception of shape which changes the listener

something in front of the flat grey ridge (<u>one</u>), not exactly

repeated in the physical presence of something next to it

1.27

pink-orange (shape) at the corner which light hits, vertical

motion of the subject whose thinking appears on the right

perception of action which (<u>is</u>) not it, the glass on a table

whose horizontal surface moves toward the following event

pale blue positioned above plane of leaves into which a bird

disappears, sound which follows the shape it arrives (<u>in</u>)

(<u>that</u>) is, location of being inside experience of the object

imagining the profile of the person in front of the glass

placement of one sound after another which doesn't (<u>picture</u>)

repeat it, where hearing happens in the space on the left

1.28

tobacco plant leaves coming back, position in the foreground

in relation to the sound of a bird which isn't the (same)

(about) visual presence of something after which it changes,

man walking toward and/or away from the memory of reading

white below blue which (is) visual, simultaneous interaction

between first and second color including experience of it

reflection of the vertical wall behind the viewer (imagined)

in back of which green continues, whose evidence isn't it

rectangular blue-green plane in lower left corner of thought

(not) exactly identical, parallel black lines for example

1.29

color moving across top of ridge, portrait and/or repetition

(<u>that</u>) is following the person in whose memory it happens

moonlit pattern of branch (<u>in</u>) shadow printed on man's waist

below the water's surface, prior to the sound which isn't

action to the left facing the viewer (<u>fact</u>), horizontal blue

line of space behind the woman whose back turns toward it

motion in relation to thinking of actual distance beyond it,

direction from which a second bird approaches (<u>calculate</u>)

(<u>a</u>) absence after which it arrives, yellow of vertical plane

adjacent to the position of right shoulder in front of it

1.30

pattern of birds against surface of plane above which clouds

(object) not moving, physical connection to second person

man behind camera facing action on left, inside wall of room

following motion of leaves in front of adjacent plane (p)

(line) between hand on edge of table and its two-dimensional

feeling, parallel to space in which the figure looks left

interior of blue square in upper right corner, (calculation)

after which thinking continues toward interior of subject

action not visible in person (defined), appearance of events

the sound of which arrives from wall in front of listener

1.31

listening to thing (<u>at</u>) exact instance of occurrence, object

which continues to be itself coming into the person's ear

surface of horizontal plane moving toward figure (direction)

crossing it, air between ridge and the edge of the window

interaction of color against white wall, whose sound follows

in relation to detail of bird landing beyond it (<u>measure</u>)

(position) before something moves to a different place, blue

square in upper left corner below which yellow disappears

gesture in which man (<u>is</u>) turning back toward second person,

transcription of thought after the shape which follows it

2.1

landscape leaning against glass in next room, memory of bird

on a telephone wire against grey-white above it (<u>present</u>)

(<u>movement</u>) of person parallel to it, light on vertical plane

beyond which the perception of blue-green space continues

angle of left leg below the water's surface before (<u>picture</u>)

actual experience, physical sensation transcribed on body

feeling extended inside the second person, followed by event

(picture) opposite surface of object in woman's left hand

action approaching the ear through which (<u>its</u>) sound becomes

thought, motion of wings descending from blue above ridge

2.2

leaves coming out on diagonal branches (d), object continued

following the woman in the car who doesn't actually speak

motion of white cloud across blue frame of sky, action (one)

hearing the pattern of sounds on a two-dimensional screen

left side of person standing at the edge of the table facing

end of second line (congruent), one thing next to another

vertical green wedge in upper left corner, bird in the green

shape of the tree in relation to memory of its (position)

(possible) feeling in the second person connected to subject

in left foreground, whose sound arrives a moment after it

2.3

shadow on vertical white wall behind performance of (action)

sound itself, whose feeling continues after it disappears

parallel to motion of green leaves, thinking of first person

following the interval between event and its (<u>antecedent</u>)

(<u>being</u>) image of figure beside the table in an upstairs room

who isn't the same man walking in a picture, for instance

second interior view (physical), blue at the end of the line

in front of plane's surface whose color isn't actually it

thinking before the object of perception (<u>that</u>) is therefore

also present, shape of the person facing an adjacent wall

360

2.4

observation of acoustic event in relation to image (<u>that</u>) is

not description, white cloud above bird's invisible sound

position of the first person not actually observed (gesture)

on the far side of the table, the object beside its sound

where horizontal line on the left stops, thought below ridge

before which yellow and/or blue next to second person (<u>p</u>)

(<u>p</u>) interior plane adjacent to feeling of the body's surface

following action, including what doesn't happen elsewhere

sound of color to the left of the door, through which figure

seems to repeat (<u>what</u>) hasn't happened in preceding scene

2.5

face turning left across shoulder, person's interior feeling

continued in the surface of color which appears to (<u>move</u>)

(<u>real</u>) events following in relation to subject in foreground

toward whom sound approaches, thinking of frame around it

man standing in front of a white rock, description of (<u>what</u>)

takes place when the second person enters woman's chamber

blue and/or white surface of landscape leaning against glass

(<u>in</u>) adjacent room, which isn't equal to experience of it

horizontal black lines next to it, perpendicular to (object)

on left whose color continues beyond subject's perception

2.6

wind-blown sand above the horizontal plane in the foreground

(here), beyond whose surface the motion of invisible blue

image of glass on a white square (there), same woman in blue

whose back turns toward window in front of adjacent plane

interaction of rectangular shapes with color opposite viewer

who sees it happen (sense), its sound moving away from it

action following previous scene, person telling the listener

how to perform something in words he doesn't (understand)

(impression) of events through the back of the opposite page

example, imagining the object in the second person's hand

2.7

vibration below surface of a leaf's tip (<u>one</u>) after the drop

falls, sound of bird imagined from behind observer's left

memory of previous action and/or the scene of action to come

seen in the corner of a flat black room, whose (<u>position</u>)

(<u>positions</u>) following the event, performance of first person

projected toward the edge of the shape which continues it

glass reflected in mirror behind it through which blue-green

light arrives, preceding (<u>sense</u>) of listener's experience

disappearance of bird in darkness of cypress branch, (<u>sense</u>)

before which something happens it doesn't actually repeat

364

2.8

green of tobacco plant leaves coming out on a branch (angle)

behind which darker mass of pine bough, ridge not visible

horizontal line between the physical object and its feeling,

followed by (how) motion of image approaches the listener

perception of subject to the right of the table which itself

disappears, blue square in corner moving toward what (is)

(position) of arm below yellow plane, whose surface suggests

dimension of an action parallel to second person thinking

relation of events beyond the grey-white (blank) to the left

of the window, the sound of whose shape will be continued

2.9

grey-white clouds moving above ridge, a feeling between blue

above horizon in the next view and white above it (angle)

(one) first person removed from scene in which woman recalls

composition of previous action, man approaching in closet

light on edge of bamboo leaf, arrival of a bird's (diagonal)

sound from perch on branch behind viewer's right shoulder

horizontal line of plane from off stage right before missing

action, that event (therefore) excluded from film version

relations between ideas of shape, (other) words for instance

color of an object moving from one perception to the next

2.10

perceived sound of acoustic dimension (abstract) as it fills

a rectangular room, before which actual motion of strings

second person facing wall, what takes place before including

(imagine) action followed by person approaching from door

three white shells on left corner of table preceded by sound

trailing off into silence, (opposite) figure moving right

blue of sky through the plane of trees, vibration of feeling

before sound crosses porch of a listener's ear (diagonal)

(system) in which the body hears, object left on window sill

remembered in terms of its color in relation to its shape

2.11

nothing above it but (<u>this</u>) space where air exists, thinking

in which paler blue-white and/or green below it intersect

close reading of closet scene, during which the first person

imagines action by the man who wants to perform it (<u>here</u>)

(<u>such</u>) as by touching her or stepping off the curb together,

example in which the observer knows something takes place

experience of other (<u>form</u>) of absence, in which the interval

between event and perception of it isn't quite determined

figure positioned on her knees in front of the man (<u>concept</u>)

taking him in her mouth, picture accompanied by its sound

2.12

silhouette of bulb's stalk standing against the window, (is)

intersected by the horizontal line of the ridge behind it

distance from body next to the person below surface of water

(calculate) not measured, candle on the table in the dark

arrangement of incidents between which space, woman on right

whose feeling becomes the third dimension above (picture)

(picture) changed to the figure remembered moving toward her

from the doorway, followed by how she approaches the pool

interior action (a) for instance, entrance of a bird's sound

from off-stage left imagined as a series of linear events

2.13

passage of a bird across the top of two windows, after which

the surface of the sky returns to its previous (position)

($\underline{x}$) equal to direction of feeling between person on the left

and the woman next to him, second person also under water

descending four-note series before (it) stops, angle of body

adjacent to the edge of the table above which map on wall

thinking continued beyond the action into which ($\underline{it}$) follows

the physical object, for example in and/or by means of it

blue square in lower left corner ($\underline{c}$), observation of subject

whose relation to the person on the right seems to change

2.14

black and white object stopped above the angle of two bodies

(glance), a performance of which action thinking makes so

motion of bamboo leaves (after) which the bird begins, whose

absence appears in physical sensation of words themselves

material presence of space beyond left window (a) not there,

as evidence of something whose feeling isn't exactly seen

cloud positioned between the top of the ridge and foreground

observation, followed by what happens in next example (x)

(b) before second person enters from the left, whose thought

continues in the relationship of subject to edge of table

2.15

person in blue walking into space across from viewer (logic)

whose experience is therefore changed, being close to her

thinking that makes nothing present, leaves starting to move

subject to condition in which something happens (example)

(man) standing next to the woman in whose previous situation

the feeling continued to shift, possibly a form of memory

performance of action, blue sky above the plane of the ridge

(measure) diagonal of whose surface seems to absorb light

how words enact a world whose meaning can't be seen or heard

for example, (how) yellow appears at upper corner of grid

2.16

sound of water falling outside and/or (picture) it resembles

in the dark, following memory of action in previous scene

face looking over left shoulder for instance, figure (being)

closer to first person subject reflected across the table

relation of the stationary object above the man on the right

to perception of it, including the other man's (position)

(position) of his fingers on her cheek, thinking which isn't

the same thing as being in the same room after she leaves

daylight coming into the picture (how) whose sound continues

connection to preceding action, silhouette of pine branch

2.17

vertical line of a drop falling from roof of adjacent house,

whose afterimage continues into the following picture (p)

(p) picture the cloud in front of the ridge, grey-white body

not moving in relation to angle of the horizontal surface

stopping at the edge of the dark rising across (description)

the bridge, which becomes the subject of the man's desire

not exactly repeated (pattern) of action, woman calling back

before the sound of the person's account of what happened

rectangular yellow feeling below a pale blue wedge above it,

(first) person's memory of coming toward a previous event

2.18

composition of a bird's motion against (<u>what</u>) grey-white sky

after which nothing, drop of water hanging on pine branch

action taking place off stage, (<u>x</u>) imagined and/or projected

which asks viewer to see something not performed in words

sound arriving across the space between its source and porch

(<u>p</u>) of listener's ear, depending on presence of something

confusion of example and its meaning, when the physical fact

that might be said to cause it isn't exactly (<u>imaginable</u>)

(<u>logic</u>) of second person's thought in relation to her desire

not to be present, memory of water in a ditch in the dark

2.19

sound of frogs in broad daylight, otherwise blue-white space

(defined) into which it may or may not actually disappear

man who watches second person stop at the edge of the stairs

having at last seen him, feel of other woman's (position)

(one) followed by what happens next, placement of right hand

which isn't therefore visible below the curve of her back

window behind the first person's left shoulder (possibility)

which faces the observer, for whom it isn't exactly there

viewed from the side (calculus), the action across the field

moving attention away from the man walking in back of her

2.20

syncopation of drops against (<u>a</u>) the horizontal plane, whose

color continues relation to feeling of vine-covered fence

woman in the green car pulling to her left (<u>one</u>) having seen

him open his door, boy in the back seat also watching him

birds calling back and forth not seen, sound which continues

whether or not the person upstairs remembers it (<u>measure</u>)

(<u>calculation</u>) of space between the breaking edge of the wave

and body moving under and/or in front of it, for instance

thought of action, followed by profile of woman at table (<u>x</u>)

parallel to something which seems to take place elsewhere

2.21

white of cloud's physical body moving across otherwise empty

blue field, below which line of ridge continues (somehow)

(imagine) bird in sight before its sound arrives, first line

followed by series of related events which also disappear

lines of face intersected by plane of the figure (condition)

standing at the end of the table, letter from man missing

leaves in motion whose sound (system) isn't physical, memory

of something falling against the upstairs window which is

observation of large baby across the room (one) who receives

his mother's attention, whose action is itself reciprocal

2.22

light refracted through drops hanging (<u>in</u>) that position, on

needles of pine bough whose sound doesn't actually arrive

man's interior feeling which appears as an object on a table

(<u>there</u>), example of pain as woman's ankle turns under her

walking across the sidewalk toward him, action (<u>geometrical</u>)

imagined as the arrangement of line and color in painting

angle of figure on the left whose momentum continues forward

interrupted by second person, who is therefore (<u>possible</u>)

(<u>condition</u>) in which memory isn't changed by it, temperature

rising when body leans back against wall behind the bench

2.23

upper edge of pink clouds (_experience_) exactly, which occurs

before the line where thinking about it becomes something

interruption of physical space continued after second person

turns back over shoulder, sees shape of object (_language_)

(_you_) meaning the figure on the right, behind whom that blue

and/or green feeling of distance one doesn't actually see

man standing in the middle of the sidewalk (_white_) as action

in street begins, girl on other man's arm not yet visible

opening the door of the car parked beside it, place in which

(_other_) person changes in relation to what happens inside

2.24

second of two doors through which (<u>confusion</u>) about the body

takes place, woman in garage whose presence isn't visible

leaning back across the room, person assuming that she (<u>saw</u>)

something which didn't actually happen to man on the left

demonstrative action of words which seem to describe subject

imagined in the following line, therefore (psychological)

(<u>attention</u>) to an empty green chair, after which his feeling

coming up behind position of horizontal figure on the bed

grey car pulling into space in front of (<u>a</u>) former location,

toward which the girl is thought to have been approaching

2.25

motion across the distance between glass and a bamboo branch

where a bird lands, which leaves before seeing (<u>possible</u>)

(<u>it</u>) happening after a viewer's perception, order of actions

reversed in the scene in which the man approaches the car

darker green wall of leaves below (<u>blue</u>) and/or white of sky

for example, a memory of the plant left on the windshield

woman thinking of actually doing that, after which the sound

(<u>effect</u>) of a bird calling back and forth in front of him

cloud moving above the line of the ridge (<u>so</u>) not repetition

of previous events, leg or shoulder below surface of pool

2.26

figure standing at the end of the table, (<u>present</u>) situation

including the sound of a different bird which isn't there

vertical lines of a building parallel to what the man thinks

(<u>position</u>) looking up at it, whereas she hasn't ever left

picture whose caption doesn't exactly (imagine) it, as event

takes place after the person across from him remembers it

plane of grey-white clouds below the blue in the upper right

corner of window on the left, memory of that (<u>experience</u>)

(example) of action which happens after it, feeling her left

leg positioned across his ankle being more than a gesture

2.27

horizontal line of ridge (<u>that</u>) isn't seeing it, after which

the sound of a bird disappears into the invisible cypress

underside of red-tailed hawk above the viewer whose distance

from his feeling about it isn't exactly clear, (describe)

(<u>how</u>) action on left occurs, the person calling on the phone

which changes the listener's experience of thought itself

two-dimensional blue of subject in upper right corner (<u>more</u>)

present than thinking of it, which isn't actually visible

leaves in motion in (<u>this</u>) line, birds in white space of sky

after which the person on the left sees child approaching

384

2.28

light moving across the surface of the water as wind arrives

(<u>describe</u>) which isn't exactly it, before and/or after it

bird landing in a bamboo thicket (<u>here</u>), picture of the girl

opening the door of a room whose location isn't disclosed

leaves in vertical crack of rock to the left of first person

walking beside it, who may not even stop to notice (<u>what</u>)

(<u>before</u>) something else takes place, the subject of the verb

whose action opens and/or closes the poppy's orange globe

black and white image of tongue (<u>function</u>) going into second

person's mouth, after which the sound of the bird leaving

3.1

condensation inside the window whose half-closed edge frames

distance of the green ridge, white next to its (<u>position</u>)

(<u>direct</u>) object on table, the experience of the first person

observer who sees it after sound of car passing in street

body of the bird on a bamboo branch (<u>not</u>) being internalized

for example, the feeling inside the subject letting it be

sitting at the table facing left, same profile of the figure

(<u>who</u>) thinking of the sight behind her seems to become it

motion of flag in field blowing from northwest (<u>like</u>) seeing

what doesn't appear, sound of two crows behind the viewer

3.2

perception of white floating in water (<u>content</u>) after action

which follows it, man walking across the room in the dark

moving toward the window (<u>form</u>) of not leaving, passion vine

behind the person's feeling at the edge of previous event

subject which appears where sound above the horizontal plane

(<u>position</u>) seems to leave, one left leg against the other

woman standing beside the table, experience of second person

facing the white wall of adjacent room's interior (<u>being</u>)

(<u>how</u>) instinct followed by the shape of next event intersect

to the left of the window, the woman walking out the door

3.3

flag draped across the air's invisible pillow, single person

(position) outside the range of feeling what's passing it

sunlight in window followed by sound it doesn't make but is,

absent as circular blue shape beside the table (<u>thinking</u>)

(<u>ear</u>) toward which two or three crows approach, darker green

silence of leaves into whose surface the image disappears

composition in the middle distance of pine needles on branch

from which a single droplet falls, one after (<u>one</u>) by one

shadows on a horizontal plane, irregular white or grey-white

clouds moving across the paler blue field above a thought

3.4

thinking the reflection in a glass surface follows its image

(optical) across room, man for example moving to the left

edge of yard (experience), moon's light on blossoming branch

memory of which continues beyond the end of the next line

perpendicular shadows on a white wall opposite sun coming up

which doesn't actually repeat, sound of a crow which (is)

(seeing) person walking to the door, identity of the pronoun

"you" becomes reading through pages of a previous thought

horizontal line of the ridge against which blue is (pulling)

viewer's eye forward, the shape of an unknown second bird

3.5

color of leaves against which darker greens, black and white

painting of a building in empty space of field (position)

(that) is followed by action of vertical lines facing a wall

which suggests a story by exploring its form, for example

grey light at the window (repeat), beyond which angle a crow

flies toward the sound of wind in trees behind the viewer

body adjacent to image between glass and landscape (picture)

leaning against it, blue-green in relation to its feeling

red visible as a thought, figure on right to whom it appears

(picture) in place of memory of person walking toward him

3.6

horizontal spectrum of an orange-pink light above (<u>reversed</u>)

unfamiliar landscape, enormous circle of rocks against it

figure facing the viewer's left (<u>one</u>), first person on phone

thinking of what the woman who called meant by doing that

particles of translucent film floating toward pool's surface

(<u>intelligible</u>) as action, new grass cutting on man's shoe

thought of how she holds a white cup, memory of crow's sound

approaching from edge of dream about the girl child (<u>not</u>)

(<u>not</u>) that an event is following the sequence from pale blue

to blinding of sunlight actually coming up, such a moment

3.7

memory of the blue-white field below vertical surface of sky

across from the viewer, whose (position) is changed by it

repeated in the following frame, glow of subject in distance

whereas what happens before it seems to be separate (act)

(or) feeling of subsequent events related by their proximity

to the first, second or third person in front of a screen

not being visible against the background, (what) takes place

opposite the sound of diagonal yellow line in back of her

angle of light source climbing above the horizon for example

(less) than equivalent to perception of it, which follows

3.8

angle of yellow lichen against the exposed surface of a rock

(<u>one</u>) at higher elevation, below which a snow-white field

followed by fog draped across top of ridge, (<u>object</u>) of verb

whose sound continues the wind passing across ear's porch

accumulation of grey-white clouds billowing above the lake's

gun-metal horizon, above which light disappears (imagine)

(example) of person looking back over shoulder, which leaves

an impression of thinking about an action after it occurs

parallel to motion of line in front of the viewer (position)

who is also moving, followed by figure in black and white

3.9

person entering the room inside the man's dream of her place

in it, which includes leaving in the dark after (pattern)

(<u>as</u>) streaks of rain coming down disappear, seeing an object

whose motion reflects color of sky before thought arrives

holding the emotion closer in the mind (picture) once action

stops, pink-white volume of a cloud whose sound continues

experience in which feeling the figure is it, therefore also

(<u>picture</u>) happening between the ridge and viewing subject

invisibility of bird behind the observer who hears it (<u>here</u>)

as present moment, blue frame above where flag is blowing

3.10

yellow square in the upper right corner of surrounding color

(<u>here</u>) whose meaning echoes its sound, which an ear hears

girl moving to couch on the wall, thinking of the person (<u>p</u>)

visible in the mirror of event he doesn't actually recall

position of man in chair (feeling) triangular to performance

of body across from her, figure in back seat not speaking

vibration of plane passing overhead, an emptiness of the air

through which the white shape of three birds moves (<u>away</u>)

(<u>is</u>) not being repeated in the composition of an explanation

of some things, yellow-green lichen on a rock being seen

3.11

relation of white to the grey-white feeling below (position)

adjacent to feeling of being inside it, person wanting it

like thought itself, his perception of trees in the distance

after which action in the vertical plane happens (_inside_)

(_one_) emotion followed by second person's experience of what

takes place elsewhere, body moving toward the closed door

flag pushed into air's hollow (fact), the acoustic dimension

whose space includes vibration of a touch after it passes

object on table relative to the girl's hand placing it there

(_significance_) prior to his seeing it, rolling toward her

3.12

horizontal line of the ridge above which blue (<u>is</u>) continued

feeling inside the object, a motion in front of its sound

figure moving diagonally across the face of the wave (<u>where</u>)

light's reflection on water's surface, perpendicular wall

memory of pink-white rose against tree, the actual red shape

between viewer and the window through which its (picture)

(position) second person in chair in front of vertical plane

not looking at it, thinking of action which happens there

presence of action (<u>that</u>) is also outside it, sound of event

approaching the moment before he happens to look up at it

3.13

back-lit shape of the person coming out of the water in grey

sunlight, blood where the accident has taken place (<u>real</u>)

(<u>after</u>) event in opposite direction, motion of a bamboo leaf

beyond which a lighter green wall whose glass reflects it

random pattern of birds in the distance moving against plane

(<u>image</u>) of white sky above the ridge, including its sound

yellow-green surface of a rock, pink-white of rose in a vase

behind which interior feeling of (<u>first</u>) person continues

presence of person (<u>p</u>) approaching in relation to the figure

whose back is turned, man at the door walking into a room

3.14

observation of tobacco plant leaves in the upper left corner

after the viewer sees it, (<u>between</u>) thinking of it and it

bird descending toward adjacent space, whose reflection (<u>is</u>)

being inside of a landscape before an action has occurred

location of feeling to the left of vertical (<u>side</u>) of memory

before its subject arrives, picture leaning against glass

child's red and/or blue jacket in a dream, figure holding it

not actually visible when person waking up sees it (<u>part</u>)

(<u>form</u>) of presence continued in enormous red mouth of flower

against window on left, whose sound isn't connected to it

3.15

position next to the feeling of being inside second person's

dream, (picture) figure behind the door after he walks in

arrangement of horizontal spaces between the color of a wall

continued in the thought of an object in front, (picture)

(it), how the arrival of its sound from across the landscape

separates light from thinking it appears to make possible

shape of trees in distance toward which a memory is extended

(under) the plane's surface, order of action for instance

opposite corner of adjacent (room), figure in the foreground

whose left arm seems to be part of what actually happens

3.16

pale blue area in the upper left corner of a grid, (<u>that</u>) is

being touched by the feeling of the object adjacent to it

sound of birds followed by bodies turning into the air below

(<u>it</u>), position of the viewer whose experience it includes

action in a previous situation recalled, person on the phone

thinking of car driving toward oncoming traffic (pattern)

(<u>is</u>) like a sequence of events taking place in upstairs room

of house perpendicular to it, person not exactly the same

apparent repetition (<u>that</u>) isn't it, approach of first light

through film of clouds whose dimension is thinking itself

3.17

approach of acoustic information at the ear's porch followed

by perception of the actual bird coming down, picture (<u>a</u>)

(<u>that</u>) isn't exactly action, the grey-green surface of water

across which the person driving the car thinks of turning

hollow space of sky into which the crow disappears (example)

in black and white memory of its absence, being continued

grey of clouds above green of leaves, motion which (happens)

adjacent to the feeling of the observer in whom it occurs

leg pulled up toward the shoulder (position) of the left arm

behind and/or under it, like an action taking place again

3.18

motion of the drop falling from the faucet which isn't (how)

it happens, but happens to coincide with what takes place

two white doors at the top of the stairs, through which girl

(is) handed from male figure to the woman who closes them

dimension of feeling above (example) of ridge whose distance

isn't seen, like sunlight passing through green of leaves

subject to the experience of the action which occurs outside

window on left, action of person at the table (calculate)

(p) in relation to a pattern of sky, clouds moving across it

whose sound is performed by an unperceived motion of wind

403

3.19

allusion to pink-white petals of rose in a vase on the table

(<u>thus</u>) in front of the viewer, which includes his feeling

doing things with words, thinking of action in adjacent room

across whose silence the shape of color and/or light (<u>is</u>)

(<u>is</u>) followed by profile of the figure parallel to the glass

plane in back of her, right hand on table not touching it

eye toward which an image approaches, white of sky that (<u>is</u>)

not actually present except for the listener who hears it

girl beside the man being like (example) the person standing

in space between an event and its feeling, whose position

3.20

grey-white fog on top of the ridge (example) from which wind

arrives, size of object depending on position of observer

yellow square in upper right corner of a grid, line of birds

(form) on telephone wire followed by an approach of sound

figure in the middle distance whose image faces an invisible

source of light, which isn't the action but (description)

(position) of person walking into the room, whose experience

includes the black and white motion of leaves on the wall

light and/or darker green surfaces of a vertical plane (one)

above which blue of sky, absence of second person implied

3.21

shape of a bird landing on branch above glass, which happens

to coincide with its disappearance in the following (act)

(is) in relation to action of being taking place in negative

space, person standing in the corner of a flat black room

figure leaning against the door, which isn't (psychological)

the actual feeling of an event in a person's memory of it

sound moving from the speaker above the listener to the wall

(that) is the reflection of the object facing it, example

color behind the observer, (his) position next to the person

whose presence occurs in the time it takes to describe it

3.22

arrival of sunlight in a window (<u>that</u>) isn't actually seeing

it occur, series of five notes after which the bird stops

landing on a vertical stalk across green of field, dimension

that (<u>is</u>) described by what appears to follow the subject

person turning his back against the empty space of an action

(<u>he</u>) continues to experience, whose perception it changes

blue above a sound's surface, second of two figures on right

before an allusion to the subject reaching her hand (<u>out</u>)

(<u>what</u>) happens after the object in the middle distance stops

being itself, again depending on position of the listener

3.23

syncopation of drops falling from roof of house, whose sound

(is) behind the color of leaves toward which action moves

other motion below the edge of irregular green and/or yellow

surfaces, perceived by person on left as notes in air (a)

(a) angle of sunlight coming into an upstairs room, her hand

balanced in front of the lower left corner of the picture

distance between the man and the horizontal plane (counting)

above which nothing, thinking followed by sound of events

figure bending over in green (essential) foreground, fingers

which appear to be holding something too small to be seen

3.24

blue in relation to yellow (<u>knowledge</u>) leaning against glass

beyond which actual green, feeling of person inside space

back of man's hand parallel to the viewer, direction of hers

(<u>interpret</u>) facing ground opposite the figure on the left

distortion of his perspective looking toward triangular wall

behind first of two figures, who means to be doing (<u>this</u>)

(<u>related</u>) example of sound itself, which follows its arrival

moving away from the thought of the person who watches it

figure on left reaching across the space of her position (<u>p</u>)

which is itself action, relation of blue to adjacent blue

3.25

feeling of line perpendicular to the vertical plane of ridge

followed by curve below it, object itself (psychological)

(figure) in front of the man whose left hand reaches forward

opposite hers, an example of previous action taking place

horizontal surface of adjacent plane tilted up (form), above

which color of grey-white sky before the observer sees it

action in which the letter being held in front of the viewer

appears to be something (understood), person beside table

memory of person walking along street, and/or which (causes)

the sound of what follows to be heard before its approach

3.26

green motion of a bamboo branch, shape of the bird (gesture)

vanishing into the moment before the viewer apprehends it

interval between an arrival of sound (action) and the object

from which it comes, how figure on right enters the dream

looking at body in foreground (position), thinking beyond it

toward an awareness of the color of light in larger space

lighter green in relation to the memory of blue above leaves

in the previous thought, arrangement of events (possible)

(thing) connected to its feeling, the shoulder of the person

closer to the vertical edge of a window out which nothing

3.27

paler blue-white plane of sky (fact), action in which viewer

in relation to subject in foreground appears to change it

pair of rocks to the right of the window followed by feeling

of the vertical line of the tree behind it, example (<u>one</u>)

(one) person driving away, palm of other's hand on the table

unconscious of the yellow rectangular plane in back of it

color of diagonal line in the right corner adjacent to (<u>his</u>)

actual thought, presence of a pink-white rose on the left

landscape leaning against glass, position of image on a wall

(<u>one</u>) which isn't the same as perception after it happens

3.28

body turning around the corner of adjacent house (position),

distance between outline of object and the feeling inside

vertical line of ridge (in) relation to its actual direction

measured from the right, the angle of the wave's approach

acoustic dimension before the sound of a bird, whose arrival

from behind the listener appears to be thus (transformed)

(expression) of person on the right reaching her hand toward

taller figure, thought of dark green tree in the distance

subject continued to the edge of white (what), light filling

the space between the vertical surface and its appearance

3.29

grey-white film of cloud before the person in the foreground

observes it, connected to action which also takes (place)

(not) the idea but an object in which it occurs, five or six

birds lined on a wire below which horizontal blue surface

shape of the cross-section of the knife (object) for example

seen from below, parallel to right leg of person in chair

girl getting out of the car in the dark, not wanting (third)

person singular to touch and/or walk around it beside her

man viewed from behind the blue face of the approaching wave

also (possible), that picture continued in the next frame

3.30

color coming into sky before the sun rises, disappears (<u>one</u>)

in cloud whose grey-white surface reflects sound of birds

how man standing at table scratches green and/or red letters

across the page, whose condition (<u>is</u>) changed by seeing it

window opening into space of (thought), which isn't actually

feeling inside the subject who watches action on the left

body face down in color pictured in terms of what the person

who claims to have witnessed it appears to say, (example)

(imagine), red mouth of an enormous flower facing the viewer

whose feeling continues to be subject to following phrase

3.31

figure entering from door on right (<u>analysis</u>), in whose hand

the emotion arrives after its yellow reddish-orange shape

diagonal and/or horizontal planes across which she continues

speaking of previous action, who appears to be (thinking)

(<u>not</u>) that the object takes place, but in air surrounding it

occupies the position of a feeling pushed out from inside

thinking of pale blue-white surface above the ridge, witness

(<u>man</u>) in background whose observation it seems to include

shadow of his shoulder reflected on white of wall behind him

(<u>there</u>) example, in which color appears as negative space

4.1

sound of water (<u>fact</u>) after the image disappears, open mouth

into which the observer imagines the space of the feeling

four orange petals arranged on the table (<u>here</u>) like thought

which happens after an event, the woman opposite the door

emptiness of color itself, black and white image interrupted

by the subject which takes place before she appears (<u>how</u>)

(being) letters in upper right corner moving toward presence

of field in which to see it, head of person in foreground

full moon falling in pale blue sky, past tense of (<u>position</u>)

feeling adjacent to the figure whose thinking she becomes

4.2

image of a physical body landing on diagonal branch observed

example, how sound comes into a picture after action (<u>is</u>)

(<u>is</u>) followed by memory of birds on the telephone wire, wind

and/or the landscape through which its feeling approaches

additional red, orange and yellow angles whose presence (<u>is</u>)

perceived to be adjacent to afterimages of the next event

reflection of the observer in relation to the object outside

window, which (<u>is</u>) itself continued in the vertical plane

placed between the person closest to light (<u>logic</u>) and shape

facing his left, two-dimensional plane in response to her

4.3

first syllable of the man's name followed by (and), or angle

from which the viewer sees man in a blue coat moving away

film of white curtain behind which horizontal action appears

to happen (so), figure on right placing hand on his thigh

line between the body of the ridge and words, (so) following

person's thought of the object on stage of previous event

intersection of figures one of whom is reflected in a mirror

behind her, the feeling of a flat black surface that (is)

(act) according to which his identity changes, woman in blue

moving from the corner toward the man who wants the knife

4.4

outside thought the motion of a bamboo leaf (<u>philosophical</u>),

the object surrounded by figures whose desire it reflects

blue and/or grey-white elevation of sky framed in a viewer's

two-dimensional feeling of being in it, isn't like (<u>this</u>)

(<u>not</u>) stopping to think, action between the object and being

the person watching the line on the floor in front of him

wind whose direction (<u>actually</u>) changes position of the flag

opposite observer, right shoulder facing center of circle

walking clockwise around it, (<u>logic</u>) of the following action

which isn't performed except in words used to describe it

4.5

direction of clouds below which the lighter grey-white (<u>one</u>)

disappearing, after sound of its shape strikes the window

first of (<u>two</u>) figures closest to the viewer, white shoulder

in front of the negative space of the person's left thigh

thinking adjacent to the yellow plane above which paler blue

appears to be continued, reflection of subject (opposite)

(<u>same</u>) person seen from inside form, horizontal line between

its vertical presence and allusion to sky above the ridge

other man placing the sound of fabric (<u>here</u>) around his legs

after sitting, starts to talk about subject preceding him

4.6

woman placed against the green wall at the front of the room

whose back isn't turned, others beginning to see it (all)

(act) in which the man takes her by the wrist, which happens

to be continued as verbal action of previous closed space

green of tobacco plant leaves changed by an approach of wind

outside window, hearing (this) sound in following picture

person who appears to be thinking it (is) not action, object

positioned above the table including her perception of it

curvature of bone on the horizontal plane (so) whose feeling

enters the space it fills, beyond a bird's acoustic event

4.7

feeling of vertical black line beside the pale yellow square

(<u>physical</u>) above left corner of table, area in back of it

transcription (<u>interpret</u>), the grey-white building of clouds

across the surface of water thought of which surrounds it

appearance of bird's invisible sound in front of the subject

who perceives (<u>it</u>) as acoustic action, being inside of it

watching what appears to happen off stage, profile of figure

whose thought includes interior of picture it fills (<u>one</u>)

(<u>this</u>) two-dimensional event continued in the shape of words

whose sound precedes them, pair of related voices outside

4.8

composition of drop falling from adjacent roof (<u>possibility</u>)

the idea of which includes its feeling, description of it

flag in field moving the wind around it, diagonal of a cloud

whose pattern appears to be part of the ridge behind (it)

(<u>that</u>) person leaning against the window beyond which actual

motion of bamboo leaves, letter in hand closest to viewer

cars stopped in the middle of the road, condition of boulder

(<u>nothing</u>) in relation to sky above the landscape above it

body of person turning around the room (<u>mechanical</u>) after he

takes her in his arms, becomes the last part of the dream

4.9

visible motion of a branch as wind passes, which itself (<u>is</u>)

the afterimage of actions in relation to a physical event

thinking after a bird's image disappears into negative space

(calculate), hearing how sound arrives inside the picture

pink-white petal in relation to the glass below it, distance

between it and the person who crosses the room (possible)

(blue) surface of the horizontal plane perceived as sunlight

outside window on the left, yellow-green lichen on a rock

color as a physical sensation (<u>observe</u>), man's point of view

framed as a vertical feeling between two figures in white

4.10

sound of a bird passing overhead followed by visible picture

in relation to it, shape heard by the viewer (phenomenon)

(you) in right foreground, person looking over left shoulder

across which feeling inside the surface appears to change

grey-white of clouds (<u>nothing</u>) which is actually an allusion

to the plane of the window, beyond which an event happens

man leaning against counter in the dark, (observer) whom she

approaches inside the memory of the action following this

body of second person next to the physical feeling around it

(experience) as a bird's shape disappears, passing window

4.11

subject moving into (position), the figure in the foreground

hearing the physical appearance of wind against back door

thought of tobacco plant leaves beyond which invisible ridge

(picture) continued, light blue in the upper right corner

profile of person facing event, hand on the table (position)

adjacent to the feeling of the pale yellow plane above it

perception of second person approaching man across the floor

followed by action, sound in relation to itself that (is)

(this) action, the arrival of sunlight through glass on left

above which the surface of the grey-white cloud continues

4.12

entrance from off-stage left of invisible bird's picture (x)

followed by another, sunlight above the shape of a branch

horizontal green space above a lighter blue square, exposure

of distance between feeling of ridge and viewer (example)

(proposition) of person between the map on the wall and edge

of table to the left, adjacent to emotion of color itself

repetition of bird's sound (system) on right, physical shape

moving against the diagonal green plane in the foreground

pair of windows through which the vertical plane of a fence

(defines) exterior space beyond it, girl calling on phone

4.13

woman calling on phone, person in bed in middle of the night

(subject) thinking of what doesn't happen inside the play

diagonal line across blue-white square in upper right corner

in front of which feeling, (exact) sense of second action

birds disppearing against grey sky, how an event takes place

before its sound actually reaches the observer (evidence)

(action) in left foreground continued whether or not the man

happens to see it, motion of flag before the wind arrives

horizontal line of arm (picture), the shadow across her face

between the material presence of an emotion and its color

429

4.14

horizontal ochre space in upper left corner, image in window

facing the man whose interior feeling continues to (<u>move</u>)

(<u>how</u>) visible appearance of bird passing through air arrives

after hearing it, sound of thinking above the second line

blue above green of leaves, relation between a bamboo branch

(position) and the vertical surface of the wall behind it

observation of a subject moving across the room (experience)

not being described, which isn't actually happening in it

action inside a grey-white field (possible), figure on right

listening to the surface of the missing person's approach

4.15

crouched in red below the wall in lower right corner (sound)

followed by birds above an adjacent field, film of clouds

thinking changes, (<u>form</u>) of the horizontal line of the ridge

after which action of flag as wind arrives from beyond it

vertical plane of the picture between (condition) of subject

and person who sees it, dark green shape of trees on left

figure in foreground extending right hand toward her, memory

arriving from the pink-whiteness of blossoms on tree (it)

(<u>it</u>) emotion of the woman calling in the middle of the night

on blue phone, color of events changed to black and white

4.16

silence followed by bird's note (<u>thus</u>), action which happens

prior to its arrival at the window to the listener's left

opposite the direction a small bird flies around in the room

viewed from the back door, which isn't exactly the (<u>same</u>)

(<u>thinking</u>) of moving through water's surface, the body being

inside the physical dimension of an event the viewer sees

off-white square in the lower corner next to space (<u>nothing</u>)

below and to the left, subject looking over left shoulder

plant left on windshield, arrival of the following (picture)

building behind which blank of grey sky above the horizon

4.17

change in the air's direction following approach of sunlight

(contrast) from across the field, shadows on a white wall

motion of the wave approaching ($\underline{x}$) for example, whose memory

continues feeling of the second person turning toward him

vertical lines on face of the building above which the woman

sits in front of the window, action of thinking (<u>defined</u>)

(<u>how</u>) it surrounds it, description of body lying on its back

preceded by sense of missing it in the corner of the yard

pink-white petals of the rose in the glass (<u>before</u>) she sees

it, which occurs after sound of an invisible bird arrives

4.18

motion of flag lifting against vertical surface of the ridge

behind it, after which thought of second action (<u>follows</u>)

(<u>gesture</u>) of woman in the green chair, whose profile appears

above the horizontal picture of the window in front of it

sound approaching from behind the listener (<u>perform</u>) as wind

passes through branches, feeling included inside an event

perception of orange moving against the green, where subject

(example) adjacent to the person seeing it seems to exist

grey-white plane of the table on top of which legs (<u>passage</u>)

appear to be changing, having come back to the same place

4.19

horizontal plane of cloud moving south (<u>position</u>) below line

between ridge and the grey-white of sky above it, thought

feeling inside the man changed, how the red-winged blackbird

comes down toward the vertical stalk (position) and stops

reflection of window glass behind the person facing the wall

(<u>picture</u>) like breathing in itself, which happens on left

blue-green surface beside vertical plane, beyond which sound

approaches from birds positioned on branch of cypress (c)

(c) sunlight arriving from across a picture outside thinking

example, like an awareness of things as they actually are

435

4.20

words above the vertical building (<u>two</u>) whose letters change

as light arrives, object on upper wall in black and white

figure walking beside the man, memory in which her left hand

feels the position left by his moving away from her (<u>now</u>)

(<u>fact</u>) subject of the previous picture which appears outside

window on right, color of flag in absence of wind's sound

yellow-green lichen on a rock (<u>possible</u>), woman in the chair

whose back is turned toward the thought of missing events

position of new moon above the ridge perceived from opposite

angle, the feeling of the figure on the right noticing it

4.21

picking up the blue phone before it rings (physical) to call

the girl who's actually calling that person, for instance

falling back into it (possible), second of two figures being

the older of the other woman's children entering on right

reflection of cup in vertical plane below which darker green

surface of distant field, viewer's face in empty (mirror)

(picture) after the subject it changes, seeing flag's motion

like hearing it intersected by the wind's invisible sound

yellow in upper right corner adjacent to which another shape

(one), whose feeling continues to be missing first person

437

4.22

pale blue of space above the field in relation to the viewer

watching position of bird change, impermanence of (shape)

(two) rocks in slow motion, sound of the first surface being

rubbed against the one below it by the person on the left

film of subject (experience) moving to the front of the room

where action takes place, black and white image on screen

wind lifting edge of flag, observer's feeling inside (frame)

reflecting the sound of an event which happens next to it

figure below the visible horizon thinking about the listener

(picture) being called, emotion following awareness of it

4.23

approach of a bird's sound before the observer sees it (out)

window on left, profile of figure standing in front of it

vertical edge beside (angle) of plane, appearance of subject

whose following perception includes the feeling inside it

sunlight in relation to thinking of the surface of the ridge

(see) adjacent to which it isn't an actual event, example

followed by object on left, the way the person's hand passes

across face in mirror leaning against the wall (imagined)

(not) like invisible action before it becomes the experience

inside thought, distance between stem in glass and viewer

439

4.24

clouds appearing to the side of the vertical building, (<u>how</u>)

it becomes the painting of what the man sees observing it

grey-white surface of background in relation to the distance

between it and absence of the ridge behind it, which (<u>is</u>)

(<u>fact</u>) in itself, physical object on the table whose feeling

seems to be continued when the listener moves to the left

sound of cars outside an image of green against a fence (<u>in</u>)

next view, the woman beside him not getting his attention

following action (<u>a</u>) above glass on left, which as it passes

changes the perceiver's memory of what happened before it

4.25

distance between edge of the horizontal surface and (<u>object</u>)

opposite the observer, whose perception seems to continue

grey-white sky in glass, man viewed in relation to the plane

above which the subject (<u>is</u>) echoed by the sound it makes

bird moving across the face of the picture above light green

tip of branch, the end of which curves below water (<u>line</u>)

(<u>that</u>) is adjacent to the listener's feeling, whose interior

dimension changes in response to the arrival of its sound

visible motion of flag in a field (<u>defined</u>) which disappears

before the person sees it, experienced as absence of wind

4.26

form of grey-white clouds above the edge of dark green ridge

for example, which the eye sees as present action (<u>think</u>)

(<u>say</u>) figure turned to the left in front of window, imagined

weight of diagonal yellow plane behind her right shoulder

relation between shape of tree in middle distance and viewer

(<u>measure</u>) who perceives it, being inside the same picture

outline of wave approaching (position), the person facing it

intersected by the sound of emotion inside previous event

pink-white to the left of the pine branch arriving in (<u>this</u>)

experience of perception itself, which doesn't include it

4.27

sound of birds passing across frame of open window (<u>present</u>)

toward action on left, adjacent to what happens beside it

right elbow resting on left knee (<u>condition</u>), inside feeling

of the subject whose back is turned toward the white wall

shadow of tobacco plant leaves on the wall behind the viewer

not moving (<u>picture</u>), in relation to actual motion inside

hand pulling through blue air, memory of the body's position

parallel to the person whose left leg isn't there (think)

(<u>think</u>) yellow square in upper right corner, object on table

continued inside the perception of the observer seeing it

4.28

figure at the top of the stairs after man walks in (<u>thought</u>)

dimension of previous room, mirror beside the yellow wall

lights of buildings outside left, the feeling of the subject

in relation to how the second person experiences it (<u>one</u>)

(<u>congruent</u>) sound of action on the right preceded by how she

picks up the phone, pale blue square in upper left corner

leaves in motion between the viewer and (<u>position</u>), parallel

lines intersected by the slope of the roof above the door

position of the woman's face adjacent to an interior feeling

(<u>act</u>) moving toward it, view of distant ridge on the left

4.29

yellow of lichen on surface of rock (action), figure on left

whose body moves below the blue plane of the next thought

motion adjacent to the bird landing on edge of branch (that)

is simultaneous action, sound of wind after it disappears

second word on top of the first, space between where meaning

occurs and the listener's perception of its sound (being)

(physical) experience of subject inside the ear whose memory

includes it, woman on the left looking over left shoulder

window blown closed (so) before its sound arrives, top right

corner whose darker blue shape seems to enact its feeling

4.30

vertical green space adjacent to the paler blue-white square

in lower left corner of next frame, for example (picture)

(gesture) person beside the table, whose interior experience

continues the color of the wall in back of an empty chair

action in the middle distance before the perceiver (p) turns

away from it, flag against which the wind blows not there

sound of bird followed by blank (description), motion of fog

across the horizontal surface to the left of the listener

second person's position (p) in relation to profile of woman

in front of pale yellow plane, whose thought continues it

5.1

grey-white band around the bird's blue-green back (<u>movement</u>)

observed from above, below which water falls into the air

thinking of body (<u>one</u>) breathing in room elsewhere, opposite

position of the man on whose left color of action happens

sound entering the listener's ear (<u>function</u>) which continues

previous perception (<u>p</u>), analysis of letters in next line

air into which water still falls, picture on left whose echo

fills the sky above the surface of a green field (figure)

(object) on the table adjacent to profile of woman beside it

feeling something, shape of silence in front of the glass

447

5.2

wind passing against the motion of a bamboo leaf whose sound

(<u>here</u>) doesn't appear in the picture, figure facing right

cloud moving south above line of the ridge, following action

adjacent to door through which she sees him leaving (<u>her</u>)

(<u>sense</u>) condition of body moving closer to the second person

under it, drop of water falling from green of pine branch

interval between previous event and her memory of it, (view)

woman whose feeling continues to change in relation to it

green stem of iris in a glass curved against plane of window

(<u>one</u>), girl walking into room preceded by sound she makes

5.3

tip of pine branch standing below plane of water's (surface)

for example, thought of lichen on a rock which follows it

flag in motion against grey-white sky, which appears to stop

(position) in relation to barely visible trees next to it

physics of sounds in concentric circles approaching listener

inside, path of a bird observed from the man's (position)

(other) action happening on the left, person on right coming

toward the memory of a body feeling something in the dark

diagonal line of right forearm (system) above which thinking

continues, cars whose sound arrives from beyond the fence

5.4

bird sound in the next room adjacent to body of the listener

who perceives it, which is inside the experience (<u>itself</u>)

(<u>what</u>) happens after light arrives, the surface of the ridge

above which brightness approaches its reflection in cloud

first person standing at the far end of the horizontal plane

(<u>situation</u>) speaking of what doesn't take place, or is it

motion of glass objects (<u>position</u>) on table, sound amplified

in the space of an acoustic event which continues feeling

pale blue field above the edge of tobacco plant leaf (blank)

which intersects it, figure coming down stairs from sleep

5.5

mosquito on a white wall (<u>angle</u>) turned red after right hand

strikes it, perception of bird passing out window on left

grey-white lines parallel to the edge of the building, shape

(<u>one</u>) picture behind the viewer facing opposite direction

distance between girl reading passage on the listener's left

and previous action (<u>calculation</u>), example of amber light

feeling inside room, condition of person in relation to body

of second child curled up under the white quilt (concept)

(picture) leaning against left corner of the window in front

of which figure sits, thinking something isn't exactly it

5.6

relation of action (<u>and</u>)/or color in lower corner, green tip

of pine branch standing up below the surface of its sound

man's hand touching the inside edge of the adjacent person's

right shoulder, intersection of lines in space (diagonal)

(<u>opposite</u>) thought of figure on left, vertical line of frame

between the angle of pale yellow plane and previous event

breathing into space below the voice part followed by person

(dimension) walking out door, coincidence of flag in wind

exact occurrence of second bird's sound (<u>system</u>), listener's

position inside the window to the right of hearing itself

5.7

two shadows at the center of a black and white plane's sound

(<u>system</u>) where the eyes were, words for something changed

vertical yellow plane on right (<u>invented</u>), woman facing left

seeing him walk toward the picture on the wall behind her

events beginning with knock at the door followed by her body

positioned across blue and/or yellow surface, like (<u>this</u>)

(<u>form</u>) of desire, color of scar on side of chest above heart

subject to the second person's memory of preceding action

man in bright blue shirt reading adjacent to light (<u>concept</u>)

example, feeling of pale blue square on the left of table

5.8

subjectivity of second person's voice arriving from in front

of a bright green square on a grey-white wall, which (_is_)

(_what_) seems to happen, sunlight passing through translucent

angle of pale green leaf adjacent to shape of its feeling

seeing the distance between the action on the left and lines

(_calculus_) next to it, body lying on sidewalk in the dark

curve of iris stalk in a glass (_picture_), woman's experience

sitting in a green chair opposite thought of watching her

physical body of the bird whose sound approaches from behind

viewer not visible, action (_a_) which takes place after it

5.9

figure seated at center of a light whose sound arrives (_one_)

following action, angle of right arm across vertical line

film of cloud which (_could_) actually exist, off-stage action

prior to the woman's appearance in the lower right corner

relation between motion whose feeling approaches the subject

(_picture_) and action beside it, pale blue light on screen

yellow rectangular shape opposite corner, beyond which white

feeling tilted against the plane of the glass behind (_it_)

(_spatial_) dimension between second of two notes and listener

who perceives it, simultaneous motion of arms on the left

5.10

one bird's sound after another, reflection of star's (shape)

a moment before the horizontal surface of the pool shifts

brightness spilling into air above the ridge in viewer's eye

after which blank, woman sleeping in the dream (position)

(is) followed by action on the right, man turning toward her

left shoulder in relation to the feeling happening inside

girl walking ahead and/or after the second person (variable)

adjacent to plane of grass, blue of water opposite viewer

repetition of action (a) stage left, door opening into space

prior to the entrance of the figure whose motion fills it

5.11

synchronicity of two birds turning in middle distance and/or

(else) disappearing, picking up the phone before it rings

picture leaning against glass (logic), the object next to it

whose vertical dimension intersects the edge of a feeling

blue square in the upper right corner adjacent to dark green

leaves behind it, sound of which arrives in like (manner)

(measure) figure standing against ground, motion of the flag

before the second person on the left turns back to see it

reflection of a white plane below dark blue thought of water

in back of the viewer, whose perception (is) thus changed

5.12

green of leaves in lower right corner in relation to feeling

next to it, where viewer isn't actually outside (picture)

(picture) sound coming forward in the dark, man next to wall

whose action continues after the second person disappears

clouds moving in front of vertical plane of ridge (position)

which is physical, yellow lichen on the surface of a rock

motion of bamboo branch as wind arrives, grey-white presence

(position) through which it approaches person watching it

blue curve of sky above the man on the right in back of whom

action of second person (position), holding left hand out

5.13

bird's sound arriving from the pine branch adjacent to house

(position) in front of listener who hears it, for example

how action happens after seeing it, the man's perception (p)

returning to the curve of the purple iris opening on left

girl passing the second person (p) opposite side of the road

in the middle distance, following the action turning back

body of the adjacent figure facing right, relation to events

after response of the man in a dark blue shirt (position)

(<u>first</u>) person moving toward subject standing in the doorway

whose hair is still wet, shape below a pale white surface

5.14

image of bird perched at the tip of a pine branch (position)

after its sound arrives, blue background of sky behind it

physical action above viewer's right shoulder, second person

moving to other side of the horizontal plane after (that)

(x) in relation to the subject toward which sunlight travels

in slow motion, feeling inside the observer changed by it

repetition of one bird sound after another in the dark, next

(view) location of blue jay's shape above the left window

person in room at the top of white stairs (logic) not absent

for instance, as a visible event becomes the next thought

5.15

light on the left above a flat black wall, presence of sound

(system) next to which listener thinks of previous action

horizontal line on the opposite wall toward which person (p)

approaches, thought of following events going on upstairs

woman moving above the man in the dark, next view looking up

performed in the space between emotion and experience (x)

(p) parallel vertical lines after which second of two shapes

also disappears, sound of next action arriving from above

pale blue behind an allusion to leaves, (calculus) of colors

repeated in the white of space below adjacent black lines

461

5.16

green dimension of tree between the viewer and blue of space

behind and/or above it, sound of speaker on the right (a)

(at) right angle to rocks on the table, dislocation of green

curve of iris passing through surface of water in a glass

person moving from the opposite room toward sense of leaving

(measure), distance from the second note to just after it

scale of breath in a vertical column (angle), drone of radio

weather after which approach of bird's sound in its place

horizontal plane of ridge beyond the pale blue-white feeling

adjacent to the subject who perceives it, (x) for example

5.17

woman standing at the end of the table, not moving (forward)

toward feeling of previous event taking place on the left

green stem curved in front of two-dimensional plane of color

(<u>logic</u>) leaning against glass, which happens before sight

sound approaching thought on right (<u>condition</u>), how listener

appears to become the image of second person's projection

motion of tobacco plant leaves adjacent to interior reaction

for example, man on telephone feeling something (perhaps)

(<u>his</u>) reflection above the blue-white plane, woman in window

whose point of view continues to shift in relation to his

5.18

vertical edge of tree against light blue field of horizontal

(one) surface, above which grey-white shape of next event

figure placed in front of rock's diagonal slope, whose sound

continues to approach the feeling happening inside (here)

(what) takes place after person on right starts turning away

from it, her idea perceived in terms of its material form

dark blue square in upper right corner, as memory (possible)

fills the wordless moments between action and consequence

yellow-green lichen on plane of rock to the right of a glass

inside which the subject (is) perceived, iris for example

5.19

curve of a bamboo branch below the angle of an adjacent roof

(<u>experience</u>), man whose perception changes feeling inside

green car passing the grey one, following thought (<u>language</u>)

in which the driver seems to lift her hand from the wheel

translucence of cloud below the horizontal line of the ridge

not exactly moving, feeling the observer is thinking (<u>of</u>)

(<u>is</u>) in relation to subject, second person's actual position

kneeling on the edge of a bed in front of figure on right

transcription of the object in (<u>other</u>) words after something

else takes place, wind lifting the lower corner of a flag

5.20

thought of person disappearing into bed of grass on the left

observed from the opposite direction, which actually (<u>is</u>)

(<u>its</u>) feeling, relation of blue square in upper right corner

to man's view of green foliage in vertical window on left

figure pointing to an opening between clouds (psychological)

moving south, below which plane of the subject approaches

shape of the iris at the top of its stalk, followed by sound

(<u>attention</u>) of an invisible bird passing memory of person

speaking of off-stage action (<u>a</u>) before second person leaves

door on left, feeling of man standing at far end of table

5.21

orange triangular shape in the upper right corner (<u>describe</u>)

followed by second action, the blue-green field around it

sound of the front gate opening, after which the viewer sees

(<u>it</u>) in relation to first person moving slowly toward him

thinking adjacent to the pale (<u>blue</u>) volume of sky above her

for instance, close-up of quail on the passion vine fence

preceded by its sound, person turning in the upstairs window

not wanting to be approached or seen by second person (<u>p</u>)

(<u>so</u>) feeling of action following what happens after he comes

back to his position beside her, yellow rose next to door

5.22

arrival of sound in front of the listener who isn't actually

(<u>present</u>), bird flitting at the wall of an adjacent house

wind moving across blue-white water's surface, figure wading

between line of thought and the opposite shore (<u>position</u>)

(<u>not</u>) the way he feels watching her change in relation to it

for example, profile facing left in front of yellow plane

motion of second person turning right, like memory of inside

(<u>experience</u>) after the physical shape of the word appears

lines parallel to the edge of a picture (theory) whose image

continues, feeling of the pale pink-white rose in a glass

5.23

diagonal motion of grey-white field approaching the observer

(then) whose feeling continues, memory of being inside it

sound below surface of glass, perception of event after (it)

stops and/or moves toward the corner of the upstairs room

subject's right hand adjacent to experience of second person

not being described, previous action happening on (right)

(is) like thinking itself, horizontal line on the other side

of which light seems to bend toward the woman in the door

green above the vertical plane beyond which cars (in) motion

which includes its sound, interior view of how she thinks

5.24

acoustic shape of bird arriving through glass above viewer's

position, next to which action an event occurs (<u>describe</u>)

(<u>here</u>) person standing against a flat black wall, peripheral

color adjacent to the listener's experience of hearing it

second person walking toward an allusion to horizontal lines

which stops (picture), starts on the far side of thinking

blue square in upper right corner, sound of subject (<u>before</u>)

feeling of absence in the house across the street changes

vertical black line above the observer's right hand on table

(opposite) it, whose perception includes being outside it

5.25

film inside the window beyond which opposite hill (position)

in grey light, feeling of buildings like shape of thought

body below the blue-green surface of approaching wave, angle

(one) shifting as it moves closer to observer's eye level

curve of actual rock on the yellow plane (not) being in same

place as its color in space, next event happening on left

two birds descending on viewer's right, how adjacent subject

intersects the back of the woman's profile below it (who)

(is) figure reflected in front of vertical glass above right

shoulder, car's sound after horizontal action in the dark

5.26

motion of invisible wind arriving from edge of bamboo leaves

(position), between the viewer and wall of adjacent house

thought followed by vertical green shape on the right, sound

leading to scale of subject in next visual scene (actual)

(position) of bird below absence of detail in grey-white sky

included in the following action, resolution of ambiguity

black rocks arranged on plane of table, first person (being)

memory of the object inside the feeling of the next event

figure looking over left shoulder (picture) whose perception

seems to continue, yellow falling into lower right corner

5.27

circle of yellow rose on the left, followed by second person

(<u>not</u>) being adjacent to the experience of seeing it occur

shape of letters in a line preceded by what he is (<u>thinking</u>)

after he leaves, composition of two bodies in green chair

bird's sound approaching listener, inside the feeling of sky

from which the echo of its sound seems to disappear (<u>ear</u>)

(<u>one</u>) side of object facing the viewer whose thought changes

watching it, surface of lighter-colored rock on the right

paler blue square in upper corner (<u>concept</u>), subject in blue

standing at the end of the table in front of a white wall

5.28

figure across the field against grey background, behind whom

feeling of a pink-white rose fills shape of window (form)

(that) is motion of green leaves on a branch wind approaches

and/or leaves, example imagined before it actually occurs

pale yellow petal falling to a table on the left, which (is)

acoustic action continued as the listener turns toward it

subject standing in front of crack in rock beyond which blue

(position) of noon, angle of thought coming toward viewer

surface of ridge below cloud (c) above which horizontal line

of final action, landscape leaning against plane of glass

                                        2.9.98 - 5.28.99